TAU LEWIS

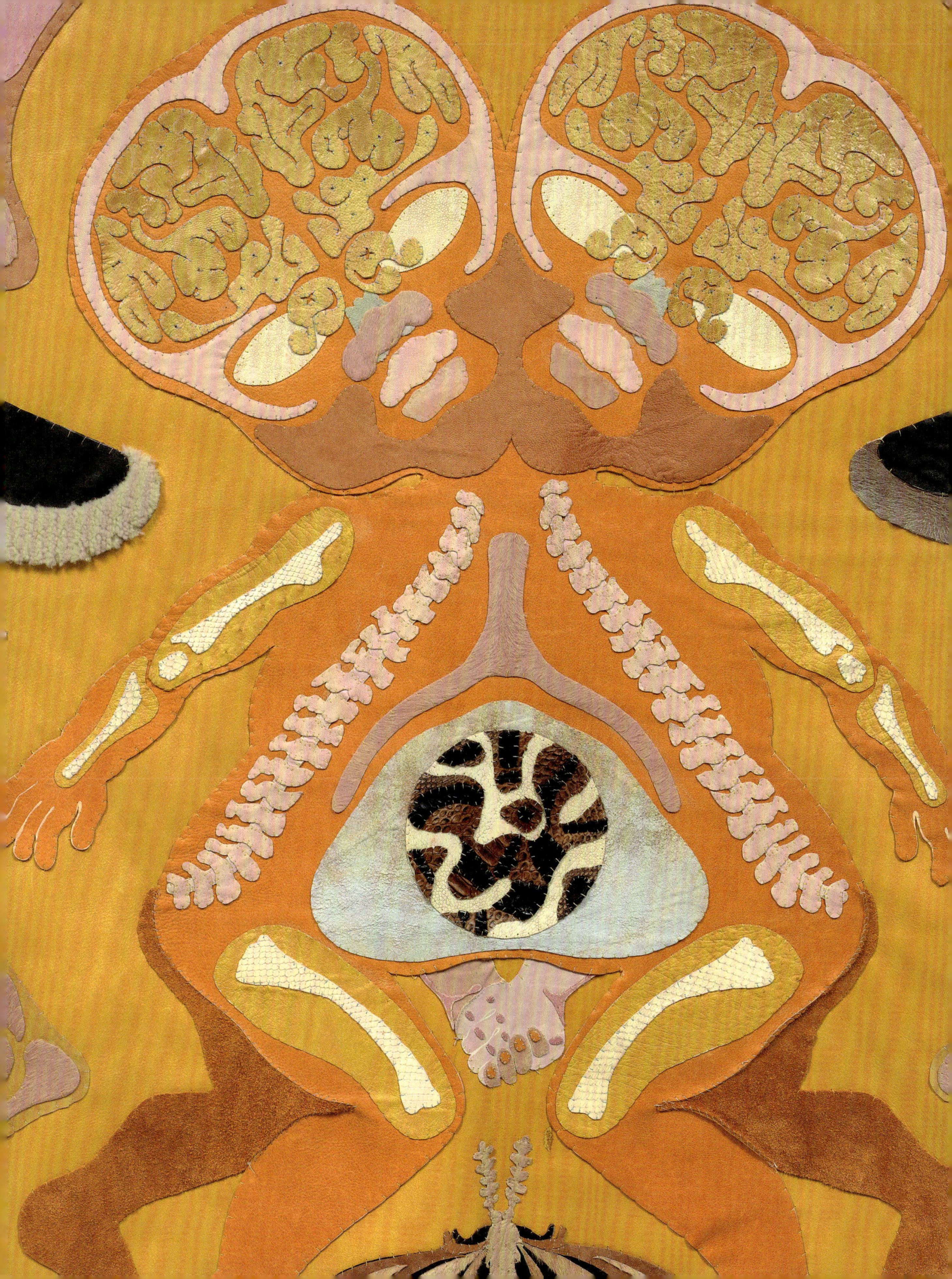

TAU LEWIS

Edited by Jeffrey De Blois

The Institute of Contemporary Art/Boston
DelMonico Books • D.A.P. New York

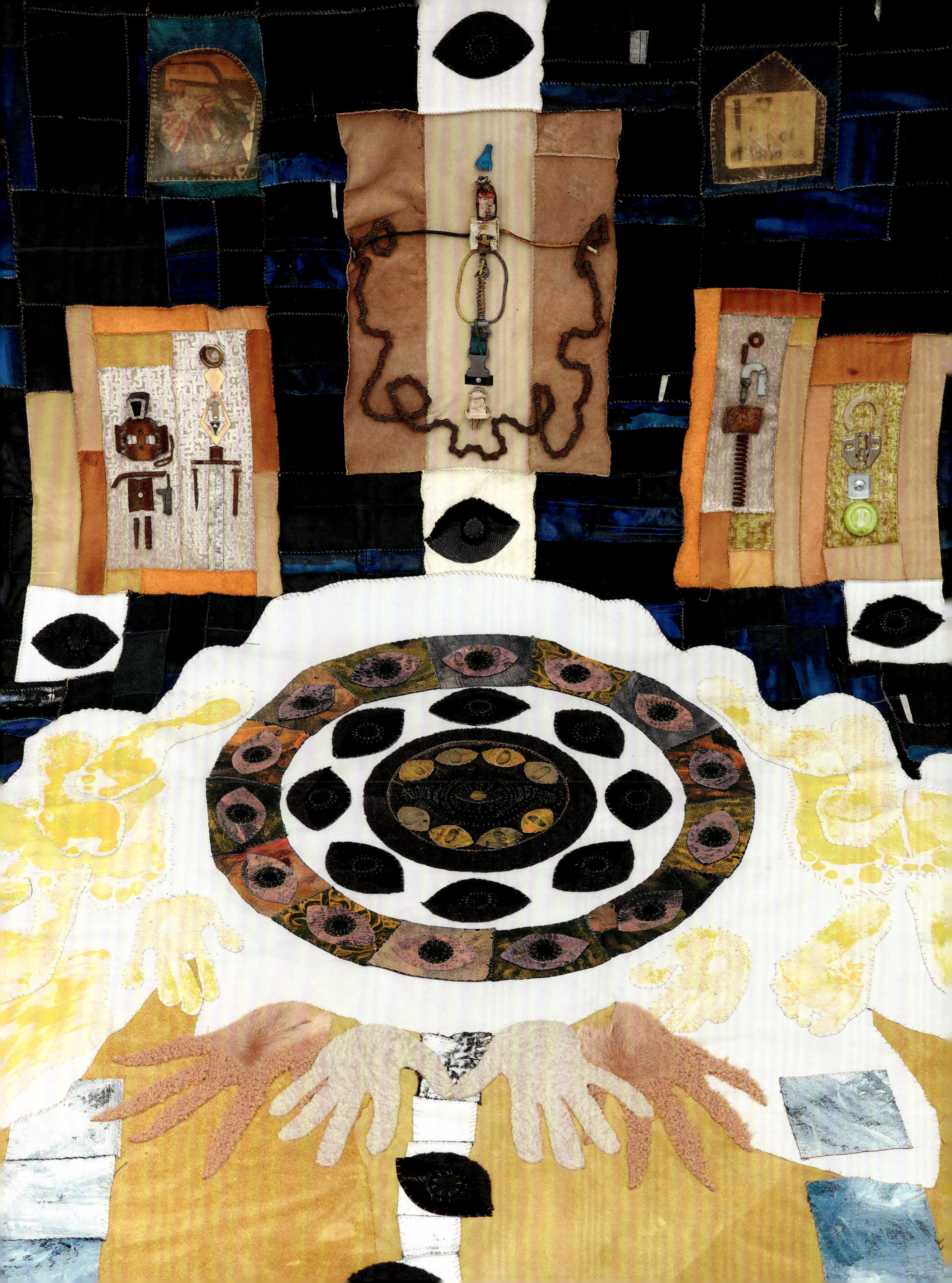

Contents

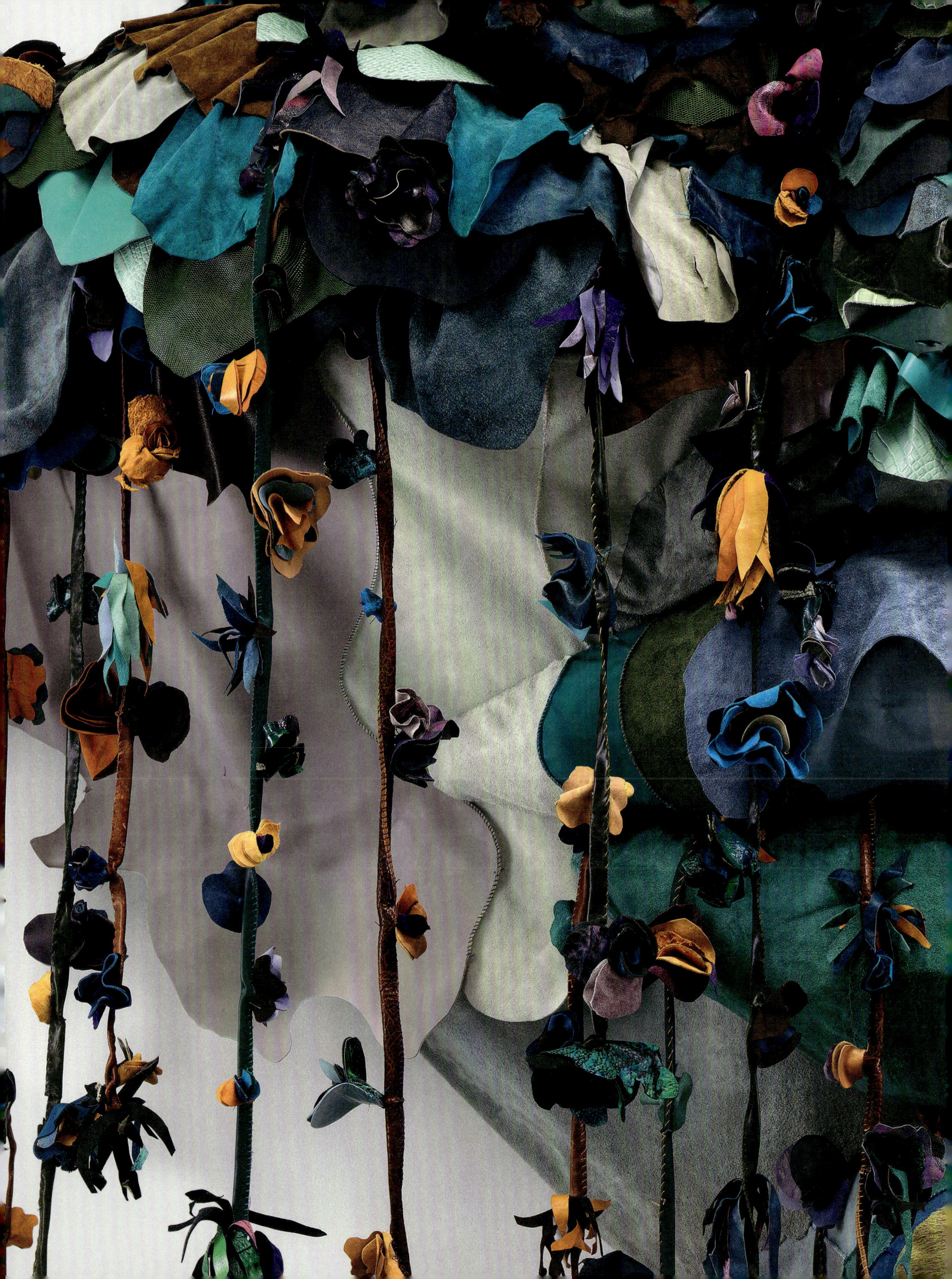

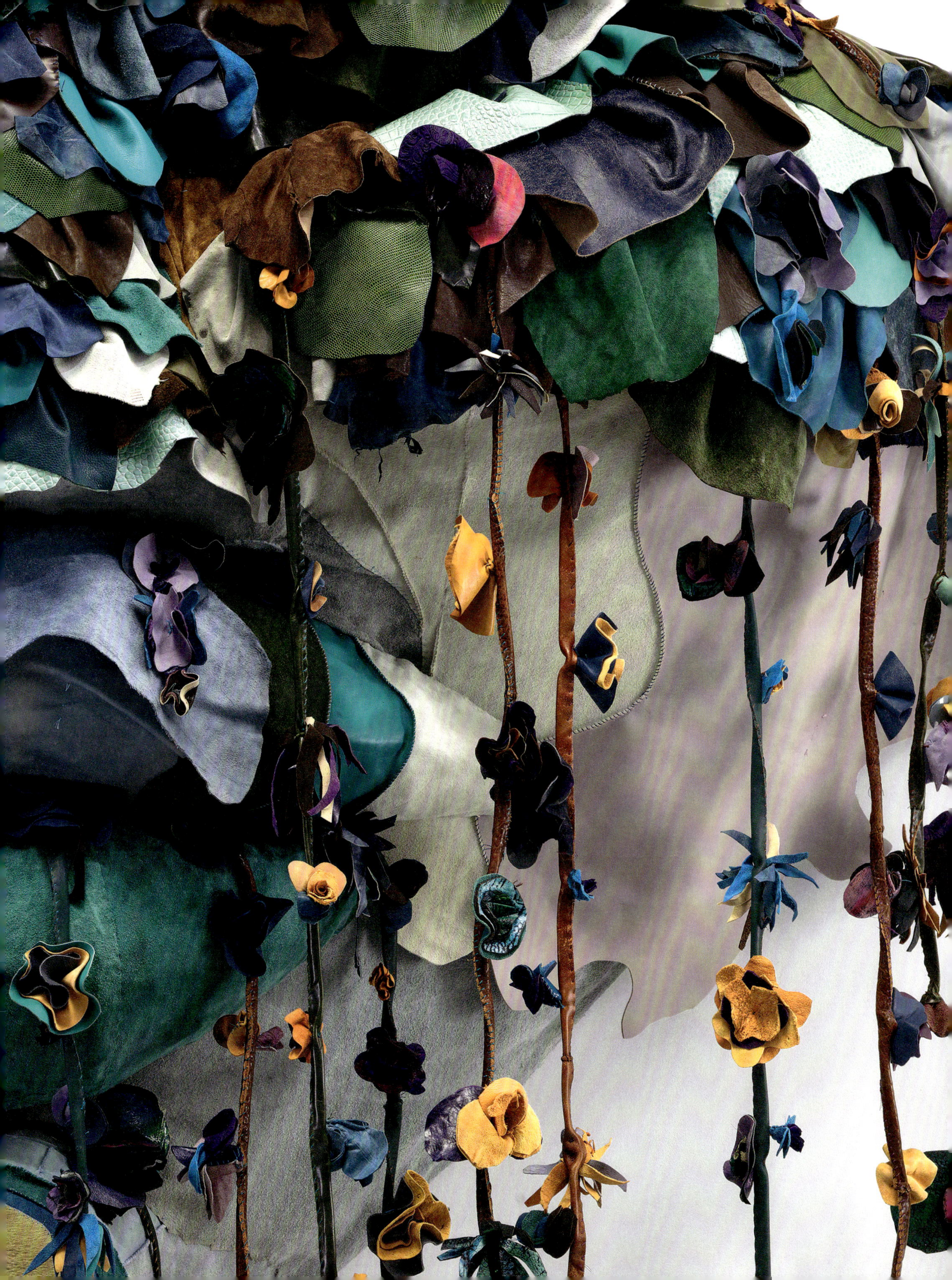

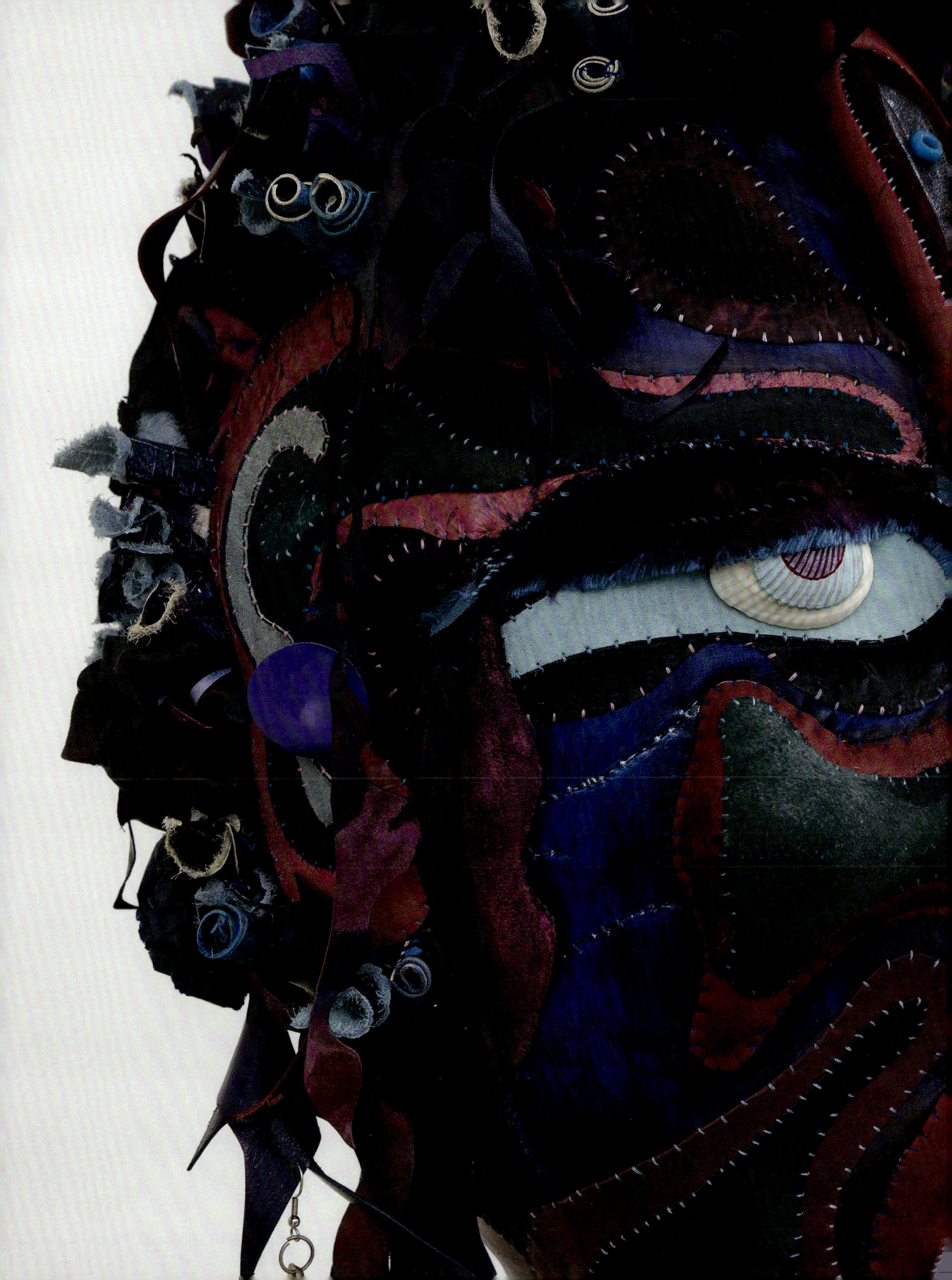

Director's Foreword

For Tau Lewis, found materials carry meaning, memory, and living histories. Lewis uses a range of art-making techniques and materials to create her sculptural work: enlargement and reduction, familiarity and dissonance, juxtaposition and collage; found and repurposed objects all serve up a powerful punch. Whether a wall-sized mask or a child-sized figure in a rocking chair, the art of Tau Lewis celebrates reparation, reuse, and reclamation.

Lewis gathers the materials for her works in Toronto, New York, and outside her family's home in Negril, Jamaica, before deftly transferring the vitality and life from one form or material to another. Her soft sculptures, quilts, masks, and intricately detailed assemblages all carry a spiritual charge, informed by the material histories they carry forward. Fabrics, leather, driftwood, seashells, well-worn clothing, photographs, and more underscore the affective power of memory and artifacts and the histories they gesture toward.

The Institute of Contemporary Art is proud to present Tau Lewis's first solo museum exhibition in the United States. We are grateful to Jeffrey De Blois, Mannion Family Curator, for bringing this idea, exhibition, and catalogue forward, and for his unwavering commitment to bringing important stories and art to our community. Jeff was ably assisted by Max Gruber, Curatorial Assistant, and supported by the ICA staff.

For their generosity in helping us realize this exhibition, we greatly appreciate Girlfriend Fund, Robert Nagle and Katherine Hein, Kim Sinatra, the Jennifer Epstein Fund for Women Artists, Miko McGinty, and the ICA board and staff. Additional support for the publication came from the Fotene Demoulas Fund for Curatorial Research and Publications.

Finally, for the opportunity to support and share her work with our audiences, we thank Tau Lewis for partnering with us on this exhibition and publication, and for the opportunity to share her unique vision and work with our visitors.

Jill Medvedow
Ellen Matilda Poss Director

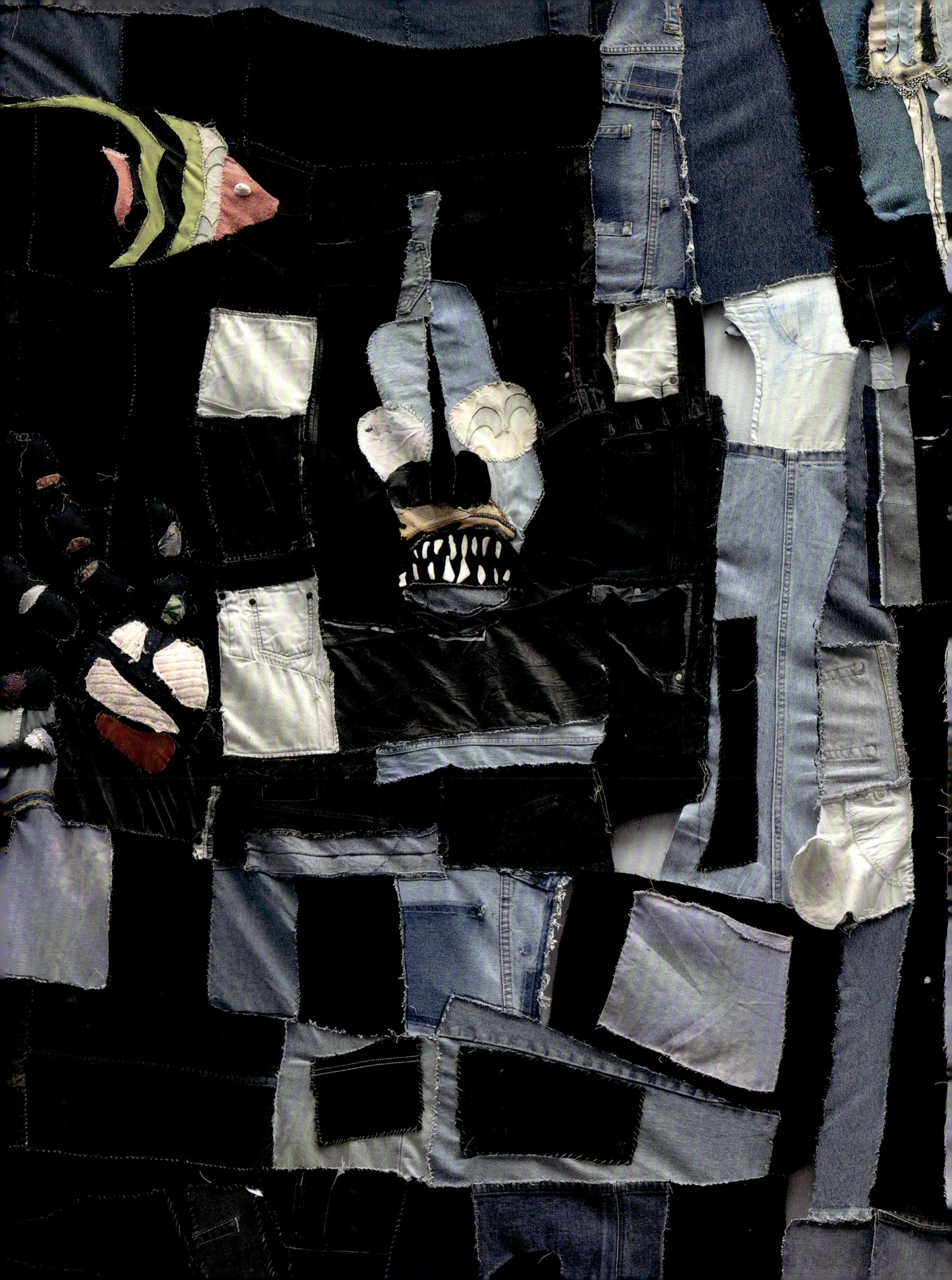

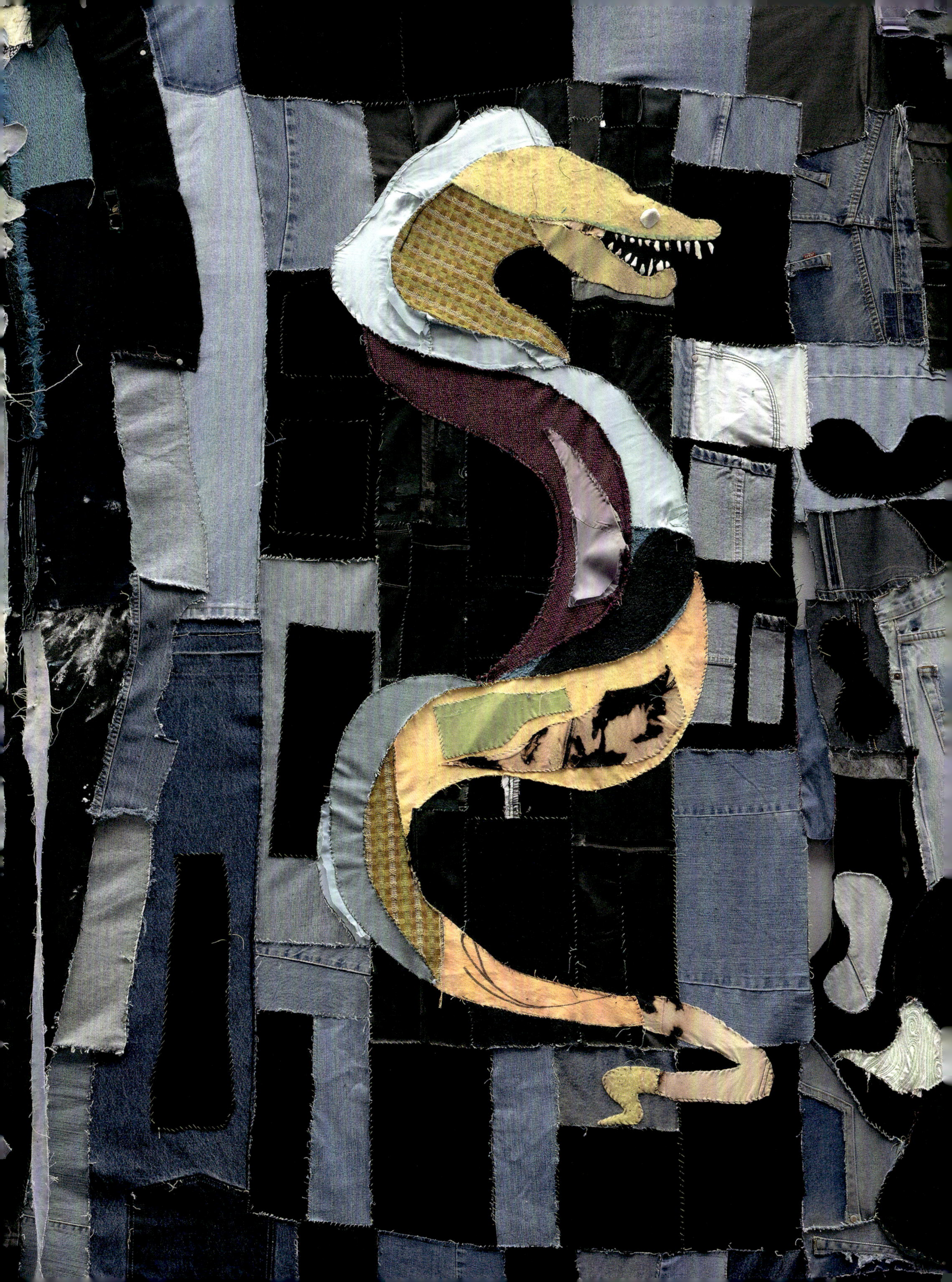

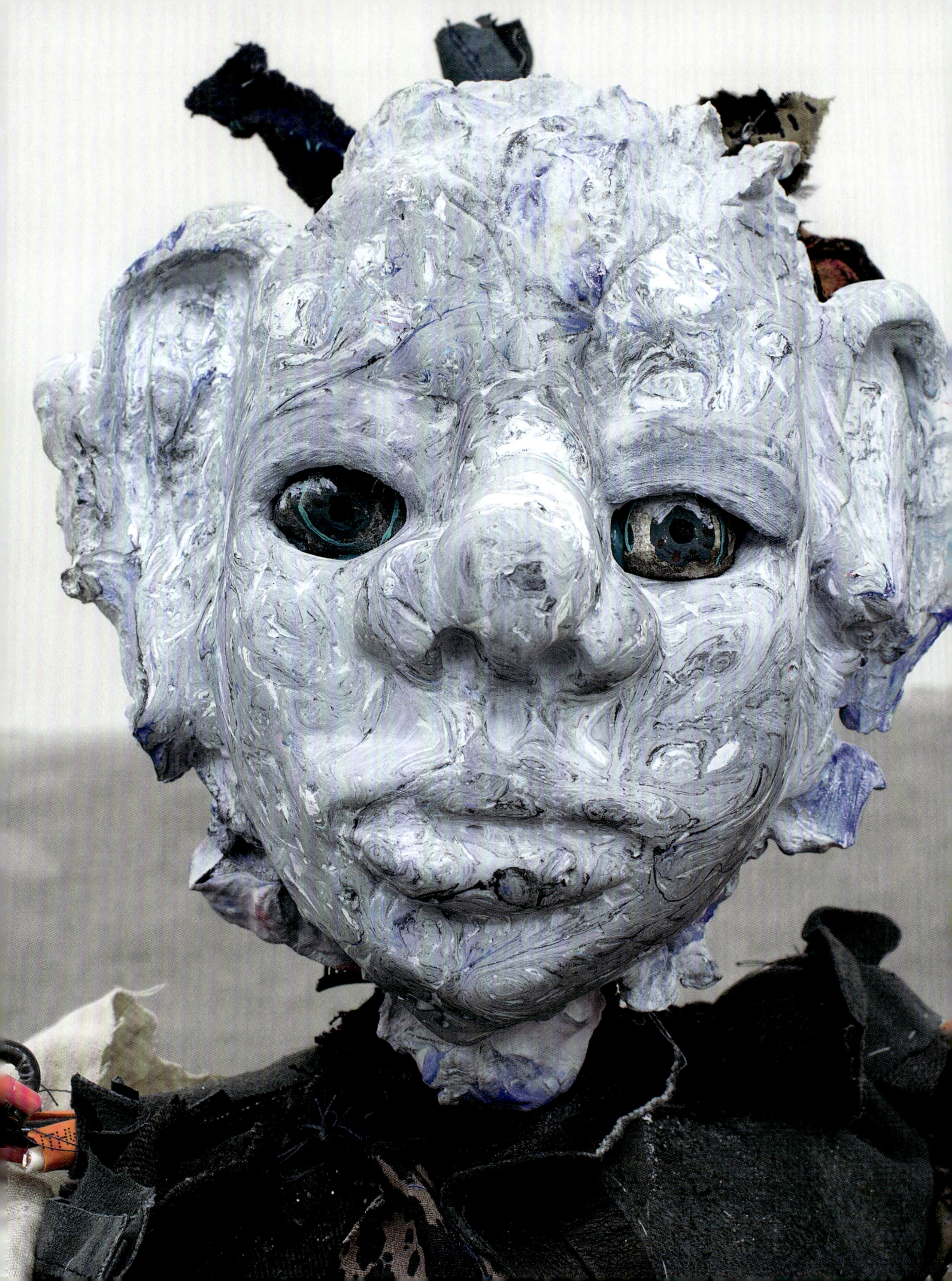

Please remember your smallness

Jeffrey De Blois

BLACK GEOGRAPHIES

The Caribbean Sea behaves like a whistle that blows so loudly it can be *heard* from space. A scientific study of the region analyzed readings taken from the bottom of the sea between 1958 and 2013 and revealed this phenomenon, named a Rossby whistle. The phenomenon takes its name from its relationship to Rossby waves, which are fundamentally different from ocean surface waves. Also known as planetary waves, "Rossby waves are huge, undulating movements of the ocean that stretch horizontally across the planet for hundreds of kilometers in a westward direction."[1] The phenomenon of the Rossby whistle was noticed in relationship to the way a Rossby wave interacts with the sea-floor in the Caribbean. Rossby waves of particular lengths die out at the western boundary of the Caribbean Sea and reappear on the eastern side of the basin, an interaction referred to as a Rossby wormhole. It takes 120 days for a wave to travel across the basin, prompting a change in the mass of the basin that registers as a rhythmic change in gravitational energy, which can be measured, or *heard*, by satellites. Although it is many octaves below the audible range, this whistle broadcasting from the bottom of the ocean to outer space plays a note of A-flat.

There is a way in which the Caribbean Sea, through this particular phenomenon and others, might be understood as a resonant body.[2] To be resonant is to continue to sound: to echo, to reverberate. Studio

Seashell (detail), 2018. Fabric, fur, leather, hand-carved plaster, acrylic paint, wire, stones, jute, hardware, seashell, and sea stones. 25 × 16 × 20 inches (63.5 × 40.6 × 50.8 cm). Private collection

13

effects such as echo and reverb are likewise foundational in dub music, the innovative electronic musical style that grew out of reggae in the late 1960s and early '70s in Jamaica. Dub—one of the most influential forms of artistic expression developed in the late twentieth century,[3] and by now synonymous in many ways with Caribbean culture—is created by significantly manipulating an existing recording.[4] The recording is material transformed into something entirely new, energy transferred and transmuted. According to musician and writer David Toop, it is "no coincidence that the nearest approximation to dub is the sonar transmit pulses, reverberations and echoes of underwater echo ranging and bioacoustics."[5]

Introducing the phenomenon of the Rossby whistle, which connects the seemingly antithetical terrains of the seafloor to outer space, in relation to dub and inspired by its "promiscuity and prolificity" as theorized by poet Alexis Pauline Gumbs,[6] begins to suggest some of the areas Tau Lewis conceives of as "Black geographies."[7] These geographies—oceanic, terrestrial, extraterrestrial—are the areas that Lewis's mythopoetic, otherworldly beings inhabit, especially as they evoke the specific forms with which she engages. These various forms, including musical styles like dub, convey the "polyphonic qualities of Black cultural expression" described by historian Paul Gilroy and associated with his notion of the Black Atlantic.[8] Lewis transforms found materials into intricately detailed assemblages, soft sculptures, quilts, and masks through intensive processes—such as hand-sewing and carving. Her works circumnavigate a broad range of references, from the mythic underwater civilization of Drexciya, to forms of material inventiveness practiced by artists such as Thornton Dial, Lonnie Holley, and the quilters from Gee's Bend, Alabama. Through the prismatic lens of the world of evocative associations she gathers, Lewis's work is directed at healing personal, collective, and historical traumas through the repetitive forms of creative labor and patterns of reuse she employs. As in dub music, found materials imbued with texture and meaning are radically transformed through a singular devotion to "the transference of energy and emotion that occurs when an object is made by hand."[9]

PRESERVATION SOCIETIES

Even though the Rossby whistle was not yet fully understood in the 1990s, it is easy to see how it would have fit hand in glove with the myth of Drexciya, conceptualized by James Stinson and Gerald Donald around

the coral reef preservation society, 2019. Denim, fabric, plaster, and seashells. 180 × 230 inches (457.2 × 584.2 cm). Love, Luck and Faith Collection

their eponymous Detroit techno group. Though their first release emerged in 1992, the liner notes penned by The Unknown Writer for the compilation *The Quest* in 1997 made their mythos explicit:

> Could it be possible for humans to breathe underwater? A foetus in its mothers [*sic*] womb is certainly alive in an aquatic environment.
>
> During the greatest holocaust the world has ever known, pregnant America-bound slaves were thrown overboard by the thousands during labor for being sick and disruptive cargo. Is it possible that they could have given birth at sea to babies that never needed air?[10]

The Drexciyan myth—"a science-fictional retelling of the Middle Passage"[11]—imagined an advanced Black Atlantean civilization as the "water-breathing, aquatically mutated descendants" of the pregnant enslaved African women thrown overboard on ships bound

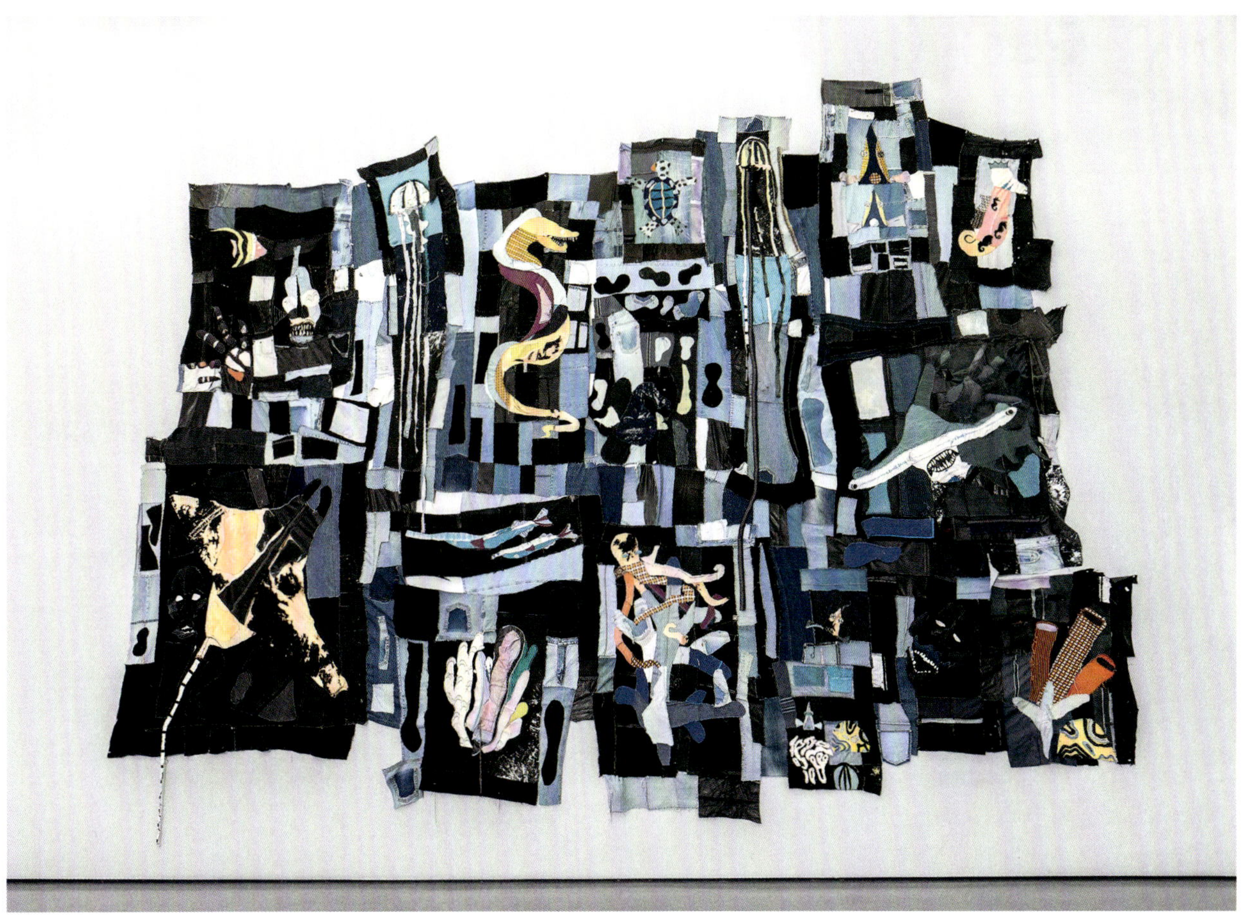

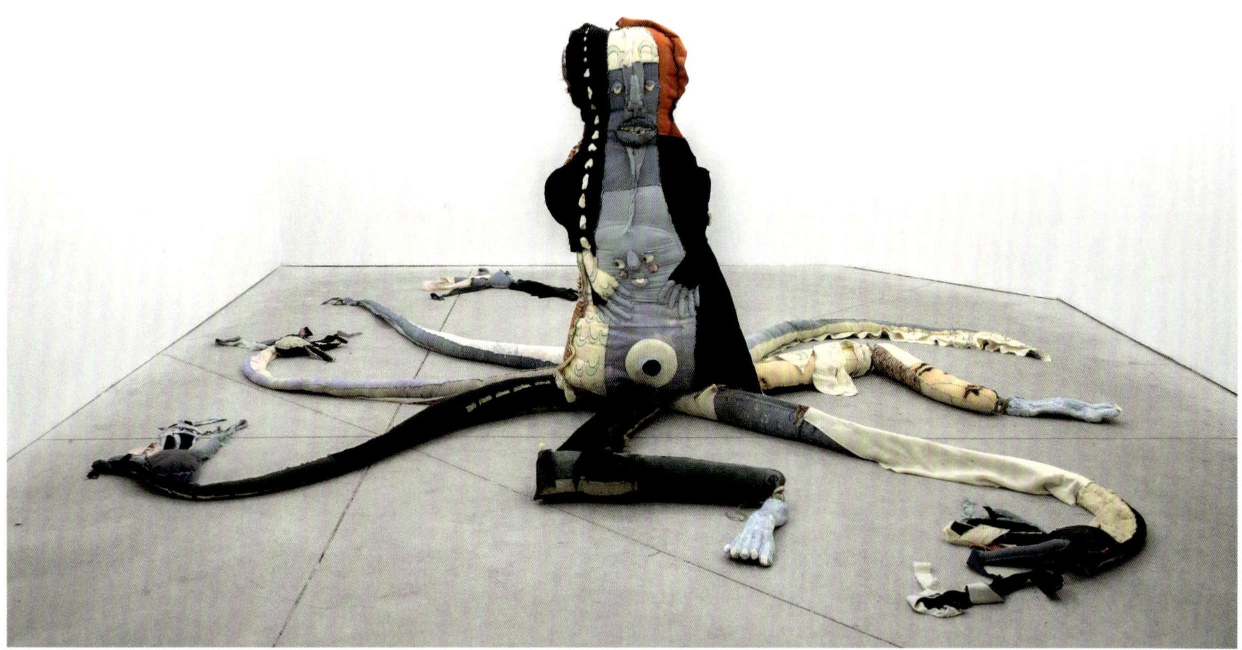

for America.[12] A densely woven narrative arc was elaborated through subsequent releases, culminating in some way with *Grava 4* (2002), described by musician and theorist DeForrest Brown Jr. as, "a sonic fiction that transports listeners to the Drexciyan home universe."[13] Like the Rossby whistle, the Drexciyan mythos stretches from the bottom of the ocean to outer space, offering to "the Black Atlantic world," according to Brown, "a message of hope and spiritual transcendence."[14]

Drexciya has had a singular influence on Lewis's creative output for years. "The saga continues to unfold," she says, "and it's the greatest gift."[15] The myth offers "submerged perspectives" (to borrow another phrase from Gumbs), which recount stories in "different voices."[16] Take *the coral reef preservation society* (2019), a tapestry-like patchwork quilt inspired by a painting that hung in Lewis's mother's bathroom. Among the moray eels, hammerhead sharks, jellyfish, and turtles pieced together from rough cuts of denim and fabric are the faces of several humanoid beings who appear to be water-breathing peoples like the Drexciyan wave jumpers. Here, ocean dwelling humanoids and sea creatures alike find society with one another, "kindred beyond taxonomy," to preserve the precious coral reef, a diverse, living ecosystem.[17]

Still other works, such as *miracle of the deep sea* (2019), imagine entirely unique figurative forms for deep-sea dwellers. Many of these works were made at a moment of sustained interest in "aquatic territo-

miracle of the deep sea, 2019. Denim, fabric, plaster, and seashells. 180 × 230 inches (457.2 × 584.2 cm). Collection of Lonti Ebers

Opposite: *Dainty the mermaid*, 2018. Fabric, fur, leather, hand-carved plaster, acrylic paint, copper pipe, polyester stuffing, wire, concrete, seashells, stones, and wooden chair. 40 × 29 × 40 inches (101.6 × 73.7 × 101.6 cm). Private collection. Courtesy the artist and Night Gallery, Los Angeles

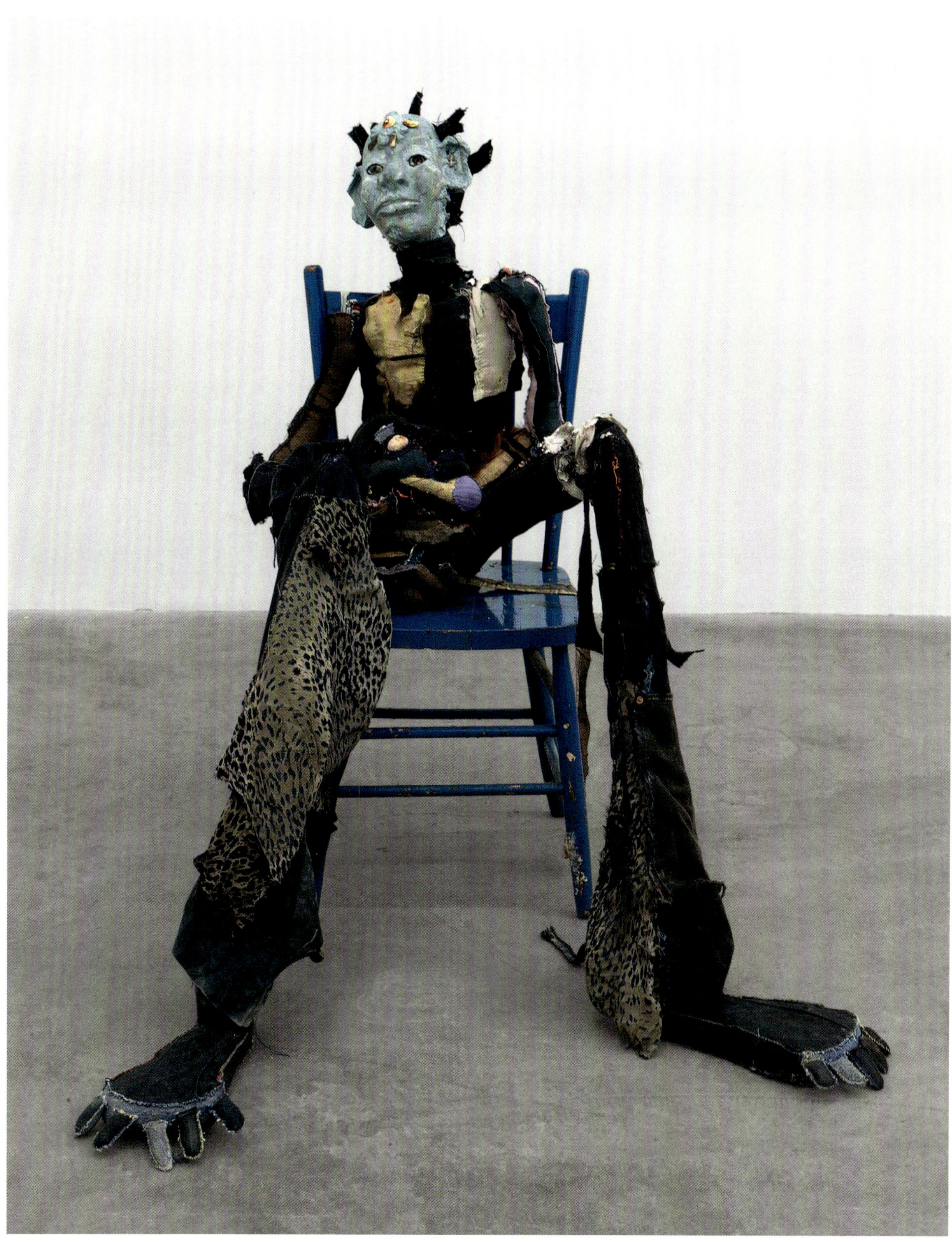

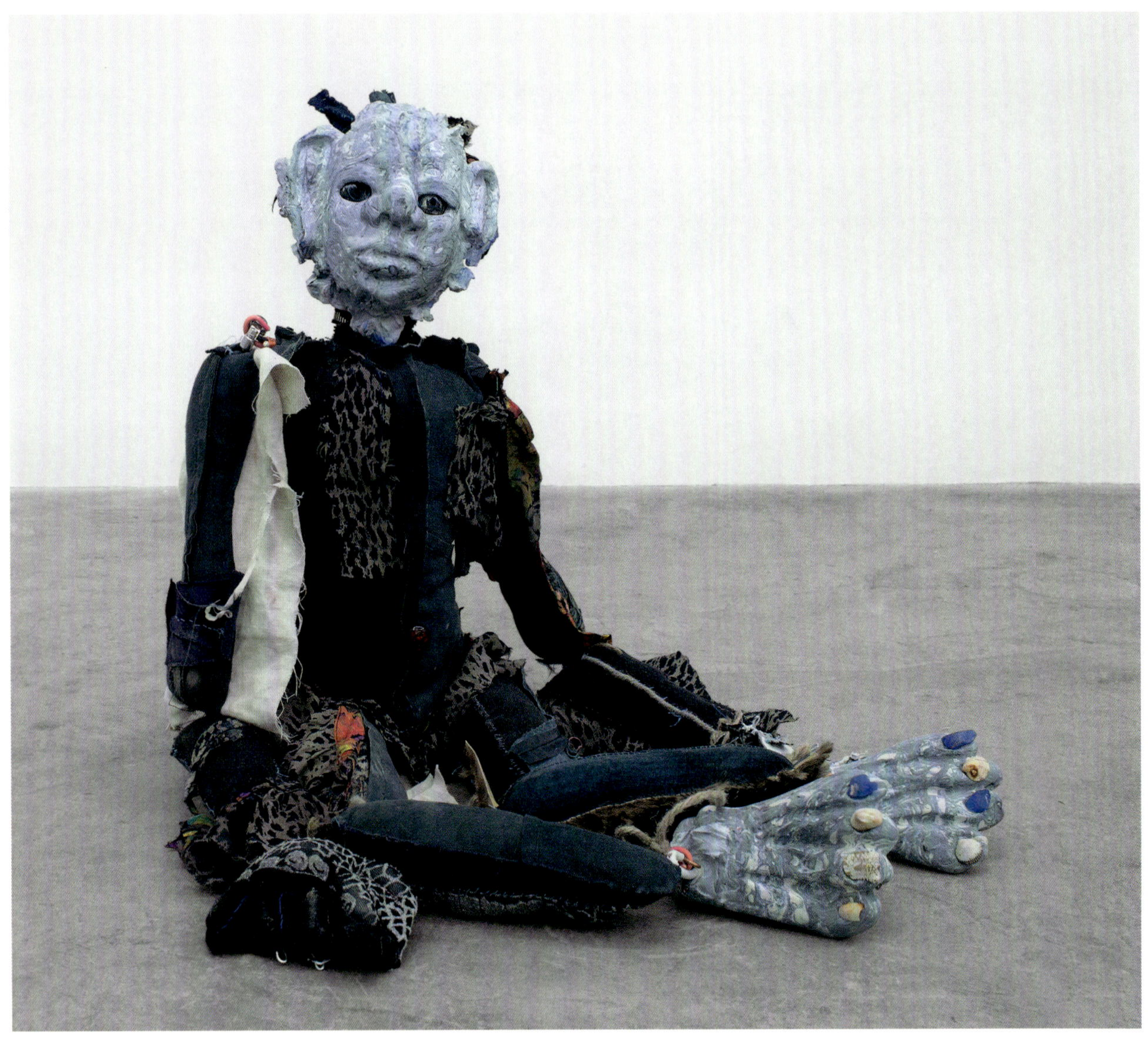

ries in relation to Black history/ancestors," according to Lewis, when the Drexciyan mythos loomed large over her work.[18] There is a way to understand the "miracle of the deep sea" as a direct reference to Drexciya, as a story of "hope and spiritual transcendence" expressed in Lewis's own aesthetic language. At the same time, Lewis sees Drexciyan wave jumpers and mermaids as interchangeable (though it is important to note that Lewis's mermaids differ from the familiar figures of folklore). Lewis's mermaids, such as *Dainty the mermaid* (2018), are physical embodiments of spirit underwater. Water absorbs spirit, and everything in the ocean is infused with a vibrating life force of which we are a part and is part of us. Her mermaids are "beings

Seashell, 2018. Fabric, fur, leather, hand-carved plaster, acrylic paint, wire, stones, jute, hardware, seashell, and sea stones. 25 × 16 × 20 inches (63.5 × 40.6 × 50.8 cm). Private collection

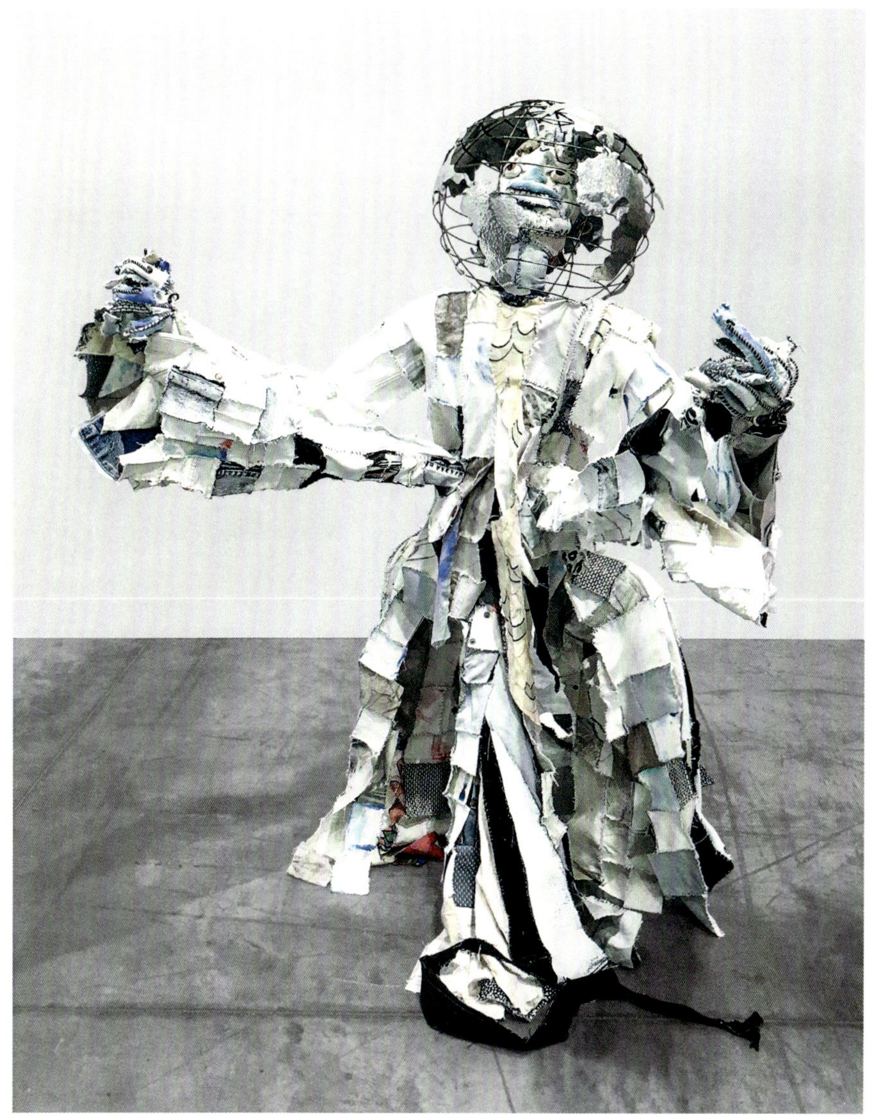

whose lives, stories, and languages were swallowed by the oceans and spat out again, becoming entities intelligible to undersea life."[19]

Lewis's visual language has always included the prominent use of seashells and other materials gathered along the shoreline (often from outside of her family's home in Negril, Jamaica), that tie her sculptures directly to the Caribbean Sea. One figure called *Seashell* (2018) composed of handsewn fabrics, hand-carved plaster, and other materials has funky looking toenails made of shell. Likewise, *The Octonaut (I can be my own hands to hold)* (2019) has shells for eyes, its head encircled by a cage-like metal globe. Even as it sees through the sea, kneeling with arms outstretched, its eyes appear fixed on the heavens above.

The Octonaut (I can be my own hands to hold), 2019. Recycled fabrics, concrete, pipe, acrylic paint, metal globe, wire, stones, seashells, plaster, hardware, and recycled polyester fibers. 51½ × 37 × 35 inches (130.8 × 94 × 88.9 cm). Collection of Josh Lilley

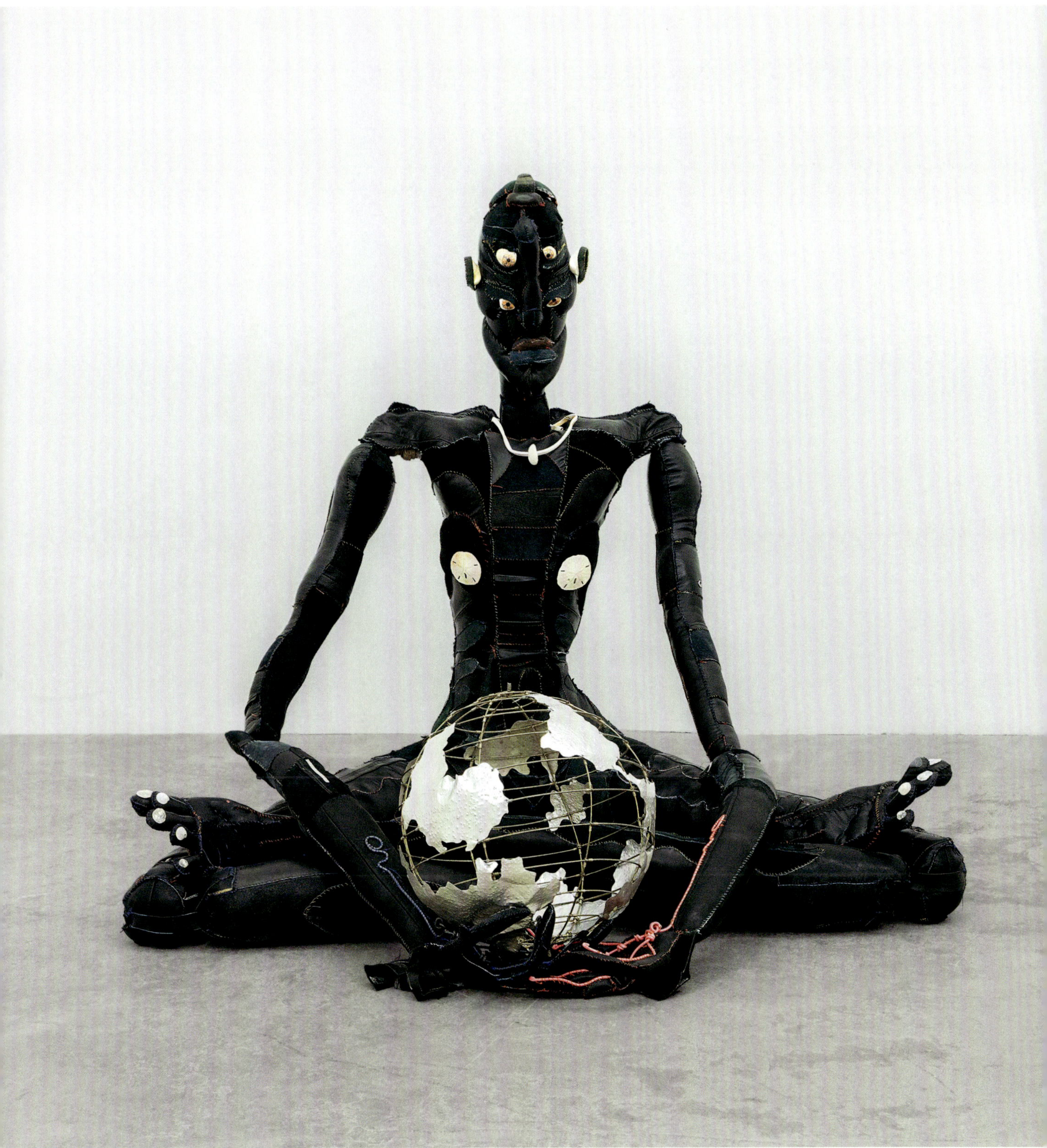

Lewis is also interested in "unfurling a sci-fi chronicle" that moves, like the return to the Drexciyan home universe, to "cosmic geographies."[20] "I look to the cosmos," she says, "as a locus of Black past and present. I'm not an Afrofuturist, I am interested in histories and the portals through which objects, voices, and allegories return to us."[21] Lewis follows the gaze of *The Octonaut* skyward to another site for otherworldly beings, such as those in her series of figures all named *Harmony*. A soft sculpture titled *Harmony* (2019), for example, is a black being made of hand-stitched recycled leather with elongated limbs sitting in lotus position. The figure holds the same metal globe that surrounds the head of *The Octonaut*, but here, there is an extraterrestrial sense of omniscience. Like its limbs, *Harmony*'s head is doubled with two faces like Janus, the animistic spirit of doorways in the mythology of ancient Rome. As in the other *Harmony* sculptures, the being's body is adorned with colorful stitchwork, with seashell eyes and sun-bleached sand dollars for nipples that stand out in contrast to their black leather bodies.

The Space Congregation (No Surprise to Find The Angels Come Here) (2019) is a large, tapestry-like work that is one of only a few works featuring found photographs. The vernacular photographs of Black women, men, and families are affixed behind semitransparent rawhide, surrounded by vignettes made of seashells, bone, and small pieces of discarded metal collected by the artist. The rawhide places the photographs at a remove; they are there and not there, part of a gathering in another place, imagined as angelic beings congregated in space as suggested by the title. This is a kind of ancestor reverence that marks their living presence, here and everywhere.

Another figure, seated with legs crossed and made of white recycled leather is called *Dumah* (2021), meaning "silence" and referencing an angel with authority over the wicked dead. Like *Harmony*, *Dumah* has a protective presence. In Lewis's cosmology, outer space is a landscape populated as much by angels as aliens, the former of which might be understood as redemptive celestial emissaries whose "true work," according to Lewis, "is to burn everything down so that it may regenerate."[22] *Three Angels Waiting* (2018) was made by combining three broken down sculptures, lending the assemblage an apocalyptic air. The angel, made from fur, leather, and fabric, appears to be bound to a cruciform structure made of concrete, rebar, and metal, and topped with an expressive length of gangly driftwood. Despite how roughhewn some of the figure's construction appears, Lewis manages

Harmony, 2019. Recycled leather, recycled polyester fibers, rebar, wire, hardware, seashells, stones, and acrylic paint. 39¾ × 47 × 35 inches (101 × 119.4 × 88.9 cm). Private collection

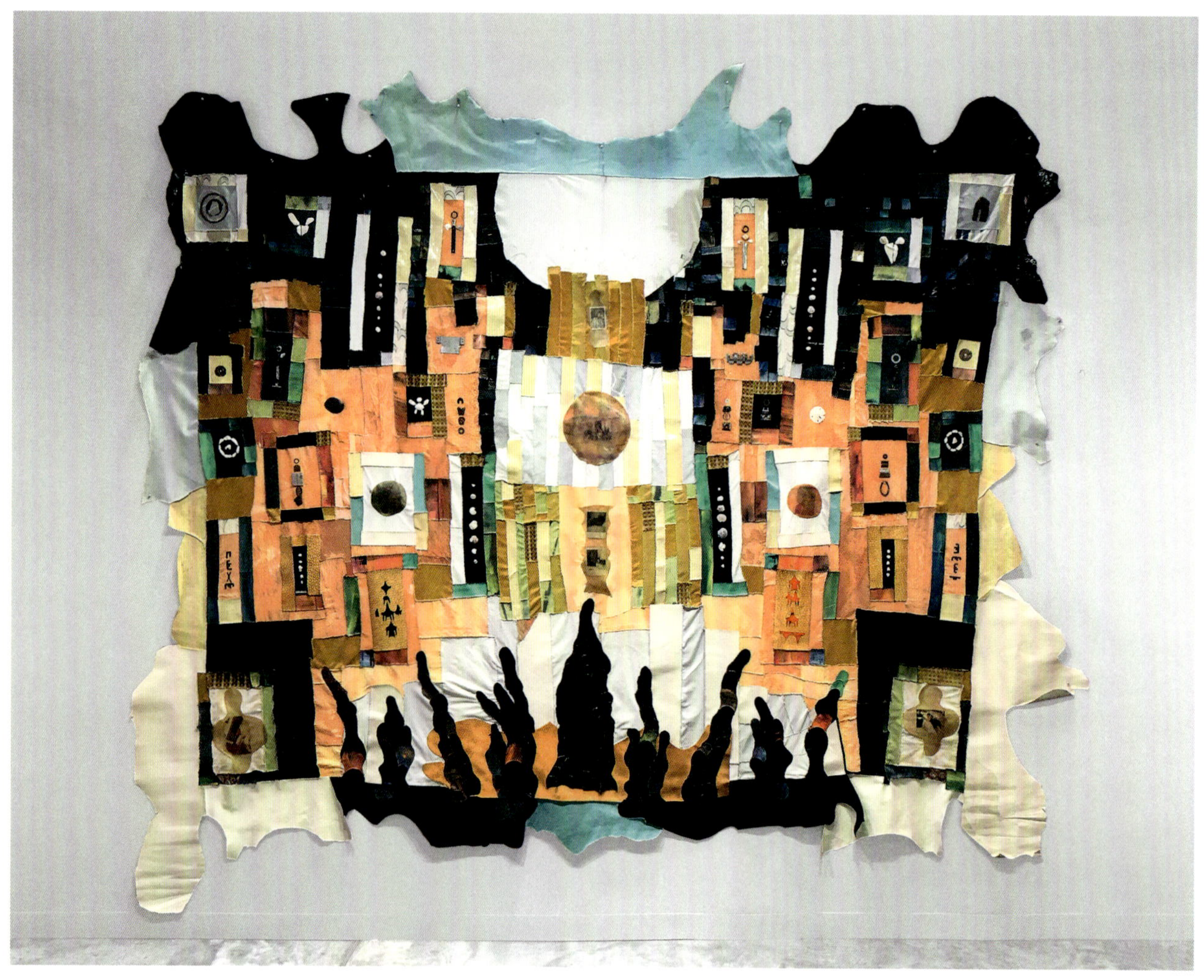

to render the angel's face with incredible complexity. As in historical depictions of enraptured divine beings, the angel's face is full of sorrow and compassion, even as it ascends to the heavens.

ENERGY TRANSFER

In 1978, Linda Goode Bryant and Marcy S. Philips published a book titled *Contextures*, one aspect of which was "to discuss, for the first time, a style that has been developing since the early 1970s which we have termed Contextures."[23] They trace a connection between artists such as Betye Saar, David Hammons, and Senga Nengudi through their use of "remains" as material in assemblage-based objects. For Goode Bryant and Philips, "remains constitute the matter of substance left over from a primary action," which they distinguish from a discard,

The Space Congregation (No Surprise to Find The Angels Come Here), 2019. Recycled leather, fabric, acrylic paint, rawhide, found photographs, found objects, bone, seashells, and stones. 120 × 156 inches (304.8 × 396.2 cm). Gochman Family Collection

whose functionality, they posit, has been nullified.[24] As it is for Lewis, music is acknowledged as an element shared between these artists, as is a certain spiritual quality of the work: "The works do not become symbols of the real or spiritual continuums, however, but rather become the transit in which these two elements co-exist."[25]

The transit between the real and the spiritual is in many ways a by-product of working with remains, materials charged with energy that is transferred in the process of working with them. For Hammons, who has worked with cut hair collected from barber shops and found bottles in predominantly Black areas like Harlem: "I was actually going crazy working with that hair so I had to stop. That's just how potent it is. You've got tons of peoples' spirits in your hands when you work with that stuff. The same with the wine bottles. A Black person's lips have touched each of these bottles, so you have to be very, very careful."[26] Likewise, when Saar outlined what she described as her "procedure" that likened her art-making to a form of ritual, she described: "The collecting, gathering, and accumulating of objects and materials, each bringing a presence, an energy (old, new, ethnic, organic). The recycling and transformation—the materials and objects are manipulated and combined with various media (paint, chalk, glue). The energy is integrated and expanded."[27]

Framing Lewis's approach to working with remains through the lens of artists like Hammons and Saar associated with "Contextures" is instructive. And yet a full picture comes into focus through a larger consideration of the artists with whom Lewis sees herself in dialog: self-taught, African American artists working with found objects, and predominantly from the American South. Lonnie Holley is one of the most influential artists in this regard. Like Hammons and Saar, Holley has discussed the energy inherent in found objects: "I dig through what other people have thrown away . . . to get the gold of it—to know that grandmother had that skillet and stood over that heat preparing that meal, so when I go home with that skillet, I've got grandmother. 'Grand': someone who has authority and is capable."[28] Holley makes explicit that the transfer of energy is a transfer of spirit.

One of several assemblages taking on the form of the cross—like so many homespun commemorative markers and graveside altars—Holley's *Grown Together in the Midst of the Foundation* (1994) is reminiscent of Lewis's *Three Angels Waiting*, though here, a cotton root's natural form lends the sculpture its cruciform shape, while steel and wire elements gesture toward the history of steel manufacturing

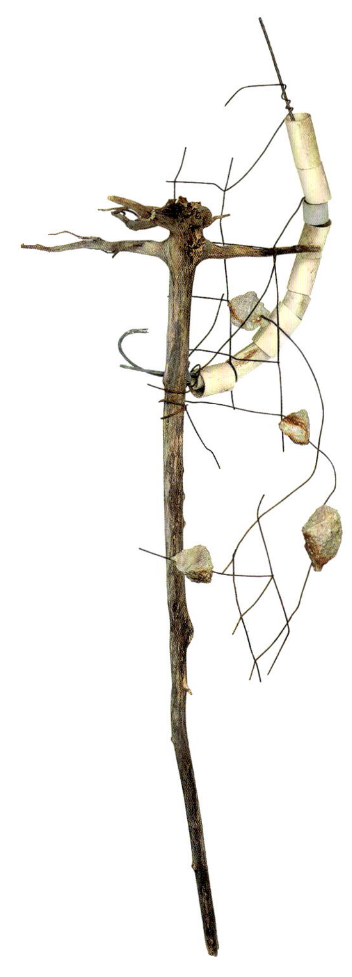

Lonnie Holley, *Grown Together in the Midst of the Foundation*, 1994. Cottonwood, steel, metal wire, concrete, and PVC pipe. 96½ × 37 × 29 inches (245.1 × 94 × 73.7 cm). The Metropolitan Museum of Art, New York; Gift of the Souls Grown Deep Foundation from the William S. Arnett Collection, 2014. © Lonnie Holley / Artists Rights Society (ARS), New York

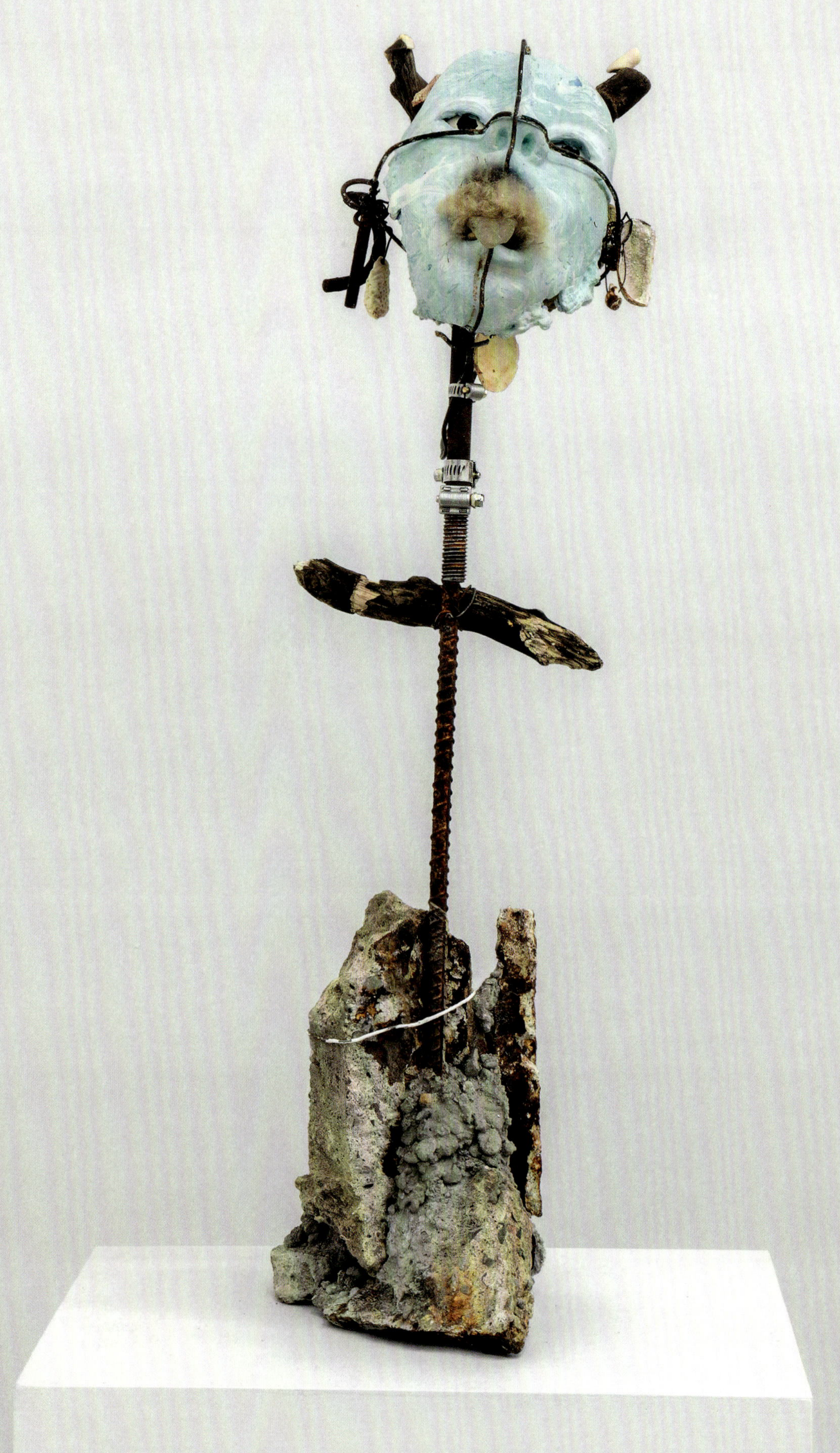

in Birmingham. Holley's assemblage suggests that slavery and steel manufacturing exist on a continuum; that Birmingham's foundation was built on exploitative forms of labor.

Whereas figuration often emerges in Holley's sculptures through a variety of means—faces made of bent metal, dolls, mannequins, and dress forms, among others—Lewis often incorporates hand-carved and painted plaster faces that make even the most abstract assemblages appear humanlike. A cruciform shape recurs in her *Precious things (everything)* (2017), as rebar rises from crumbling concrete and is crossed with a small piece of driftwood. A turquoise-marbled face of carved plaster sits atop the rebar with bent metal that traces the contours of the face in profile, much like how Holley manipulates similar material. The backside of the head, whose shape is suggested by the bent metal face, holds the "precious things" suggested in the title: delicate and beautiful pieces of reef stone, seashells, and sea glass that seem to suggest that this is a being who apprehends knowledge through an understanding of the interconnectedness of all things.

Other of Lewis's assemblages employ the form of a hand-carved, painted plaster face in an assemblage of concrete and rebar, such as *Seashell (grinner)*, *Heartbeat (quiet thrum)*, and *Big tooth (angels in a sleepy current)* (all 2017). Each of these works conveys not just how expertly Lewis works with found objects, but also how adept she is at carving expressive faces out of plaster. These faces, even as they look worn, degraded, or otherwise distressed, appear to transcend their circumstances. They are knowing, full of the kind of wisdom and honesty sometimes associated with children.

Boom bang (shiny girl) and *Baby bumblebee (for the betterment of us all please remember your smallness)* (both 2018) are figurative sculptures that are both smaller in stature. *Boom bang*'s face and hands are made of carved plaster, their patchwork body constructed of rough-cut pieces of fabric sewed together. They sit directly on the floor, holding a metal chain like the one used in *Big tooth* fixed around the neck of a found miniature rhinoceros made from wood. The figure's head is topped with dried flowers, and moving toward the rear a tail becomes visible, as does a dirty doll. Their hair is made from various materials, including—suggestively—a long lock of hair cut from the artist's head.

Baby bumblebee, like *Boom bang*, has a plaster face topped with dried flowers. Unlike *Boom bang*, however, whose face stares straight ahead, unmoved, *Baby bumblebee* wears a gentle smile. They sit

Precious things (everything), 2017. Hand-carved plaster, stone, brick, reef stone, seashells, sea glass, milk thistle seeds, wire, acrylic paint, driftwood, rebar, and concrete. Dimensions unknown. Collection of Christine and Murray Quinn

Back: *Boom bang (shiny girl)*, 2018. Fabric, fur, leather, hand-carved plaster, acrylic paint, wire, stones, jute, hardware, human hair, found toy, leather gloves, wood sculpture, chain, and dried flowers. 20 × 16 × 20 inches (50.8 × 40.6 × 50.8 cm). Collection of Dean Valentine and Amy Adelson

Front: *Baby bumblebee (for the betterment of us all please remember your smallness)*, 2018. Fabric, fur, leather, hand-carved plaster, acrylic paint, wire, stones, dried flowers, concrete, glass ball, salt and pepper shakers, and cotton batting. 16 × 18 × 18 inches (40.6 × 45.7 × 45.7 cm). Private collection

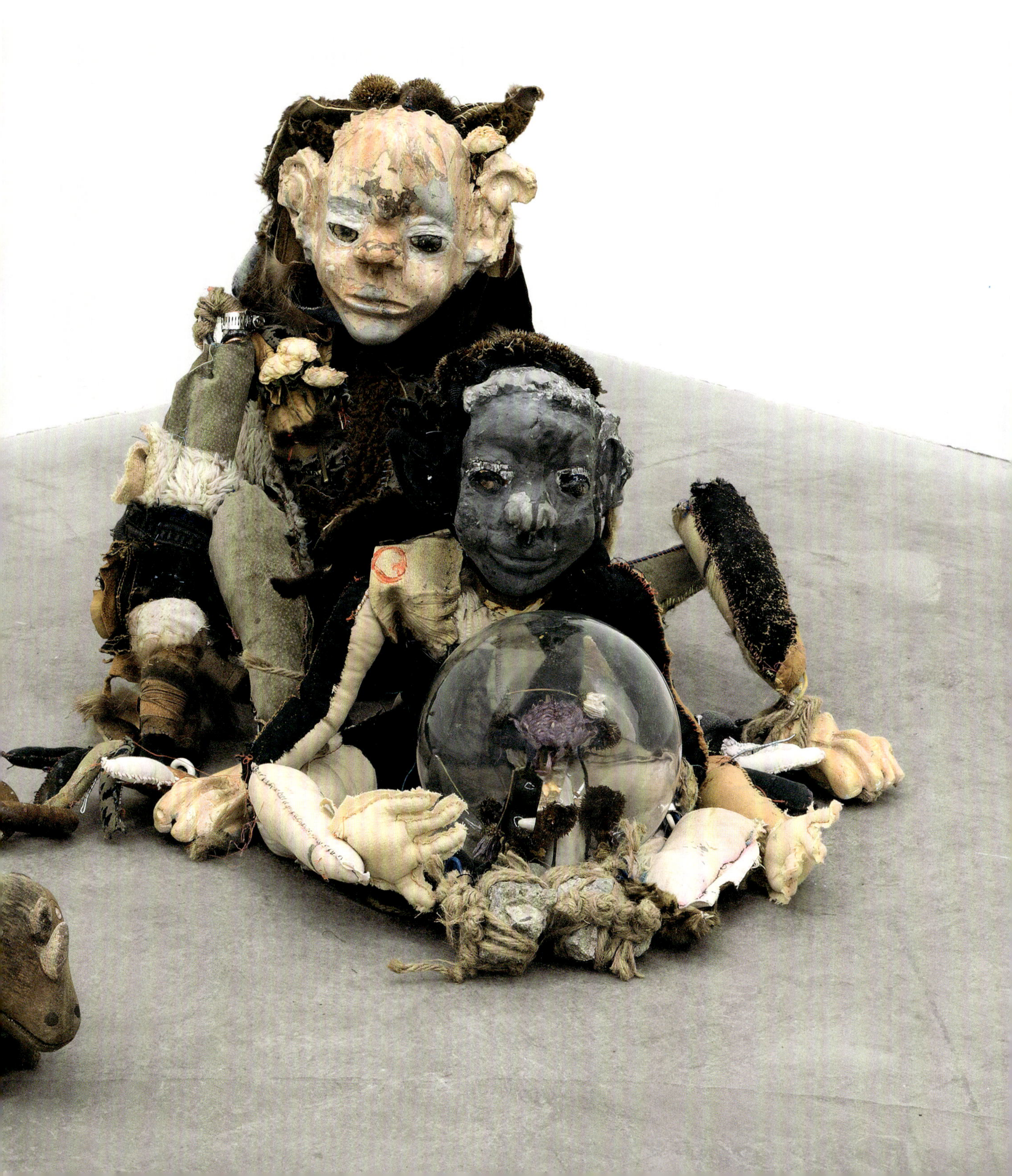

holding a terrarium-like glass ball that houses various dried flowers and black-and-white salt and pepper shakers. Rather than a tail, *Baby bumblebee* has wings, even though they sit earthbound directly on the floor. Their wisdom is self-contained, like the objects in the terrarium. They remember their smallness.

As with Holley, a central aspect of Lewis's creative practice is embedding secret objects within her sculptures. These are objects of personal significance, including written messages or lines of poetry, sometimes acknowledged in the list of materials related to a work. Most often it is an intimate aspect of the work that Lewis keeps to herself. For scholar Katherine McKittrick, hidden objects suggest hidden ways of being. "In many ways, conceptualizing blackness as a way of unknowing is an enunciation of black life and livingness pre-cisely because those in power cannot always profit from what they cannot see and grab up. There are things they cannot have. There are things we can keep to ourselves. We can keep some love hidden. We can keep the song, the story, the heartbreak, the notebook, hidden."[29] This is emblematized in some way by Lewis when she says, "everything is a time capsule."[30] The time capsule is a deliberate method of com-municating with people in the future. If one of her sculptures was to be opened, the hidden heart would be revealed, radiating energy. And yet these objects are hidden intentionally, a protective measure through which Lewis can always hold their energy close.

THE POETICS OF SOFTNESS

When Lewis met Holley in Atlanta in 2018, where he has lived since 2010, their connection was immediate. Holley offered advice to the younger artist, including one piece that ended up being consequential: "You have to do it like Mr. Dial."[31] Holley was talking about his friend and fellow self-taught artist Thornton Dial, who had passed away two years earlier. Holley was encouraging Lewis to incorporate found fab-rics in her work in greater depth.

Dial's work in found object assemblage combined a radical diver-sity of materials imbued with great symbolic power. He employed a variety of approaches to working with fabrics, sometimes adhered to canvas on wall-based assemblages, at other times as part of tower-ing sculptures, such as *Freedom Cloth* (2015). One of several homages to the quilters of Gee's Bend (several of whom Dial met in 2001), *Freedom Cloth* is a large, mound-like object topped by coat hangers wrapped in rags to "symbolize the women of the community whose transformation of castaway cloth into quilts afforded them expressive freedom."[32] Like Dial, the quilters of Gee's Bend have been a touch-stone for Lewis, who even connected with Essie Bendolph Pettway, a third-generation Gee's Bend quilter. Reflecting on their conversation, Lewis found that she and Pettway have shared interests in working with found fabric: "We're really thinking deeply about the ghosts that are in the materials."[33]

Following Holley's advice and the influence of Dial and the quilters at Gee's Bend, fabric became Lewis's primary material for creating quilts, soft sculptures, and monumentally scaled masks. In 2018 Lewis began making patchwork quilts, including some whose rough-cut,

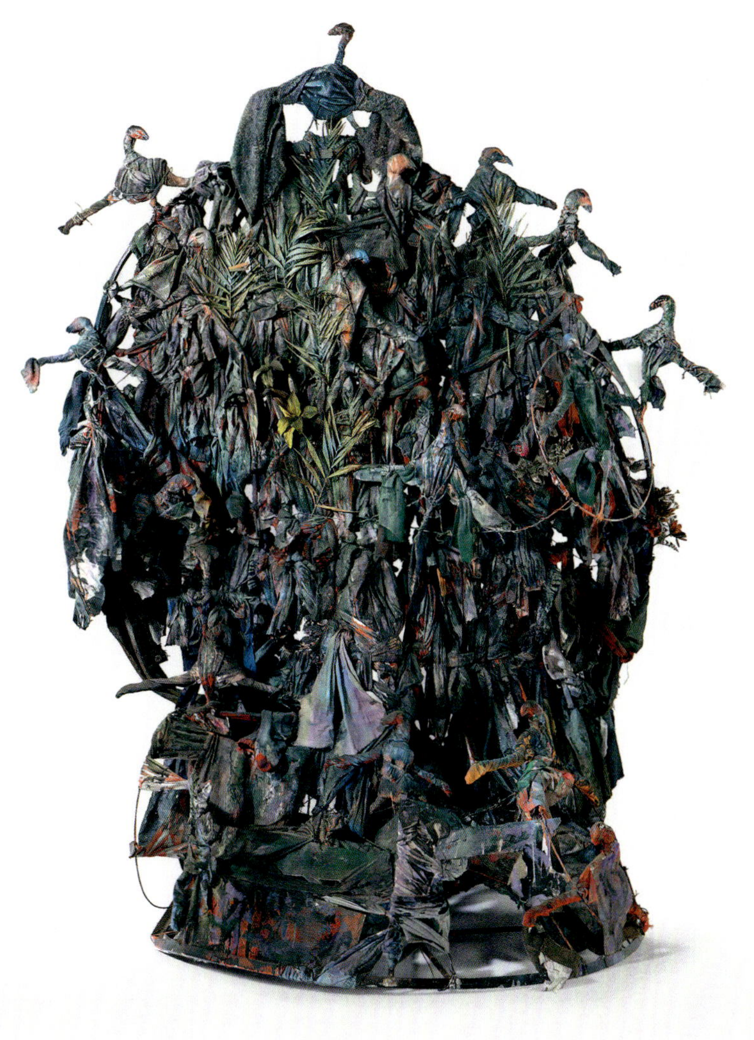

Thornton Dial, *Freedom Cloth*, 2005. Cloth, coat hangers, steel, wire, artificial plants and flowers, enamel, and spray paint. 86 × 68 × 57 inches (218.4 × 172.7 × 144.8 cm). Courtesy Souls Grown Deep, The Thornton Dial Estate

handsewn forms foreshadow *the coral reef preservation society*. Like
The Space Congregation, *Ascension of the Holy Vessel (Be Not Afraid)*
(2020) is a wall-based quilt that combines stitched and painted or
dyed fragments of fabric, found photographs encased behind rawhide and recalling objects fossilized in amber, and makeshift accumu-
lations of metal objects foraged mostly from urban environments.
In *Ascension*, the structure is architectural: the quilt has a geometric,
pyramidal shape that becomes less rigidly organized and more
organically shaped as it spills onto the floor. The upward thrust of
the work from the floor to the top of the quilt suggests the ascension
of the title, and the way in which the Black vernacular photographs
reflect Lewis's notion that angels were once real people, staring back
at the viewer (potentially, even, through the various eyes emblazoned
on the quilt).

A large eye stares out from *Knot of Pacification* (2021), a quilt
whose shape derives from a colorful hide of leather. A pacification knot
(or, *mpatapo*) is an adinkra symbol from West Africa for reconciliation.
Here, reconciliation is suggested through two childlike figures holding
hands and whose bodies are fused, flanked on either side by large
wings like those of a butterfly just below the figures. *The seed of the
wawa tree* (2020) references another adinkra symbol, this time one
that stands for toughness and perseverance. Two pregnant figures,
one black and one white, hold hands and gaze at the other's pregnant
belly, a black baby in the white figure's belly, a white baby in the black
figure's belly. The brown leather background is adorned with several
adinkra symbols, including the Funtumfunefu Denkyemfunefu, which
stands for "unity in diversity given a common destiny," and Akoma
Ntoaso, "the joining of hearts."[34] *Knot of Pacification* and *The seed of
the wawa tree* both draw on traditional wisdom conveyed through
distinctive symbols, given rich and meaningful expression through
Lewis's tapestry-like quilts.

By now a signature aspect of Lewis's practice are the soft sculptures
she refers to as "soft portraits," figurative sculptures whose appear-
ances range from the roughhewn character of *Boom bang (shiny girl)* to
the finely detailed needlework of *Harmony*. These portraits evoke a
"poetics of softness," to borrow a phrase from art historian Max Kozloff.
While much has certainly changed since Kozloff was writing about Claes
Oldenburg in the late 1960s, the title of his essay is poignant, as is his
notion that "regardless of how abstract a soft sculpture is, it will
unavoidably evoke the human."[35]

*Ascension of the Holy Vessel
(Be Not Afraid)*, 2020. Recycled
leather and fabric, acrylic paint,
rawhide, found photographs,
found objects, bone, seashells,
and stones. 216 × 108 inches
(548.6 × 274.3 cm). Hammer
Museum, Los Angeles. Pur-
chased through the Board of
Advisors Acquisition Fund

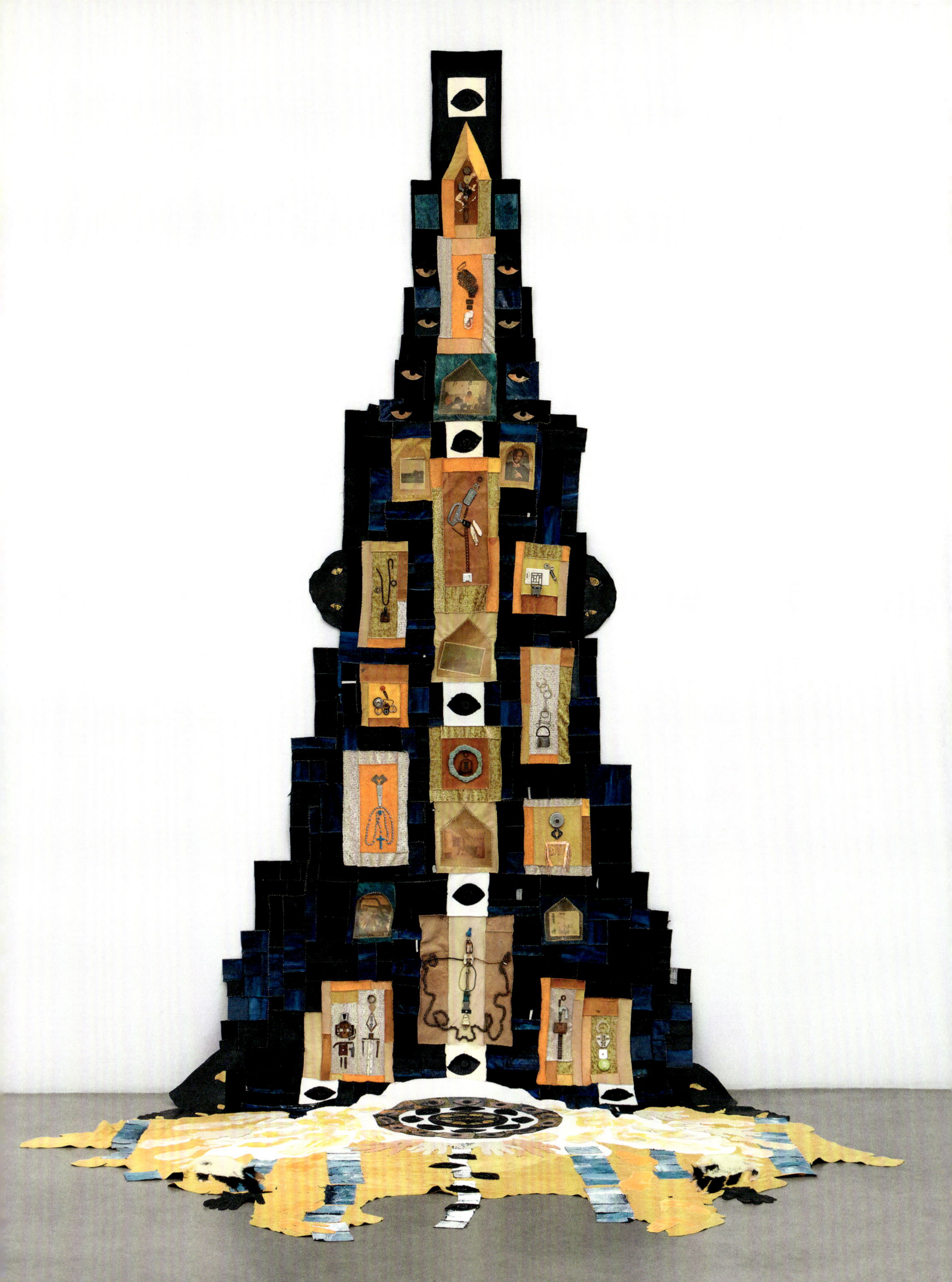

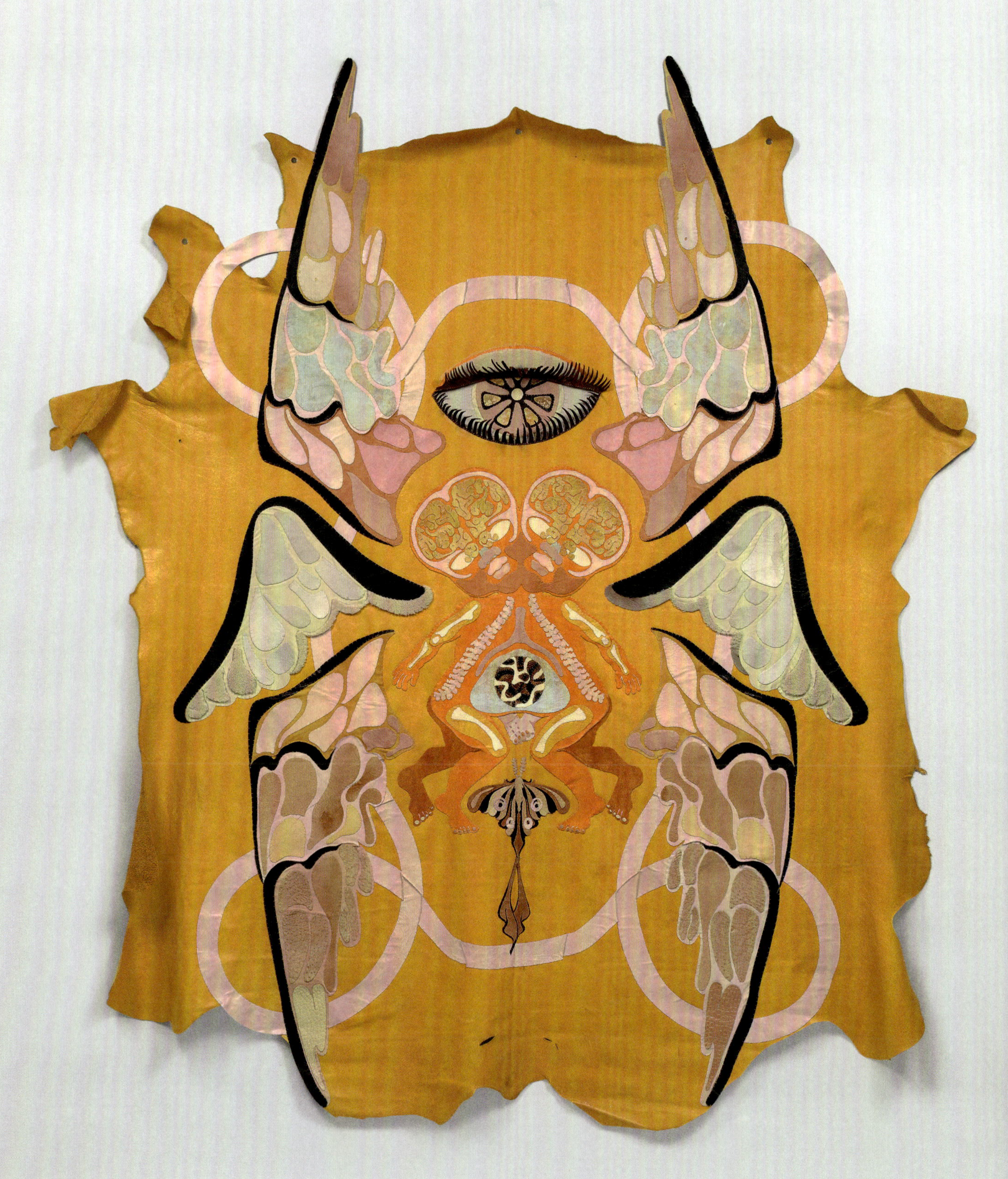

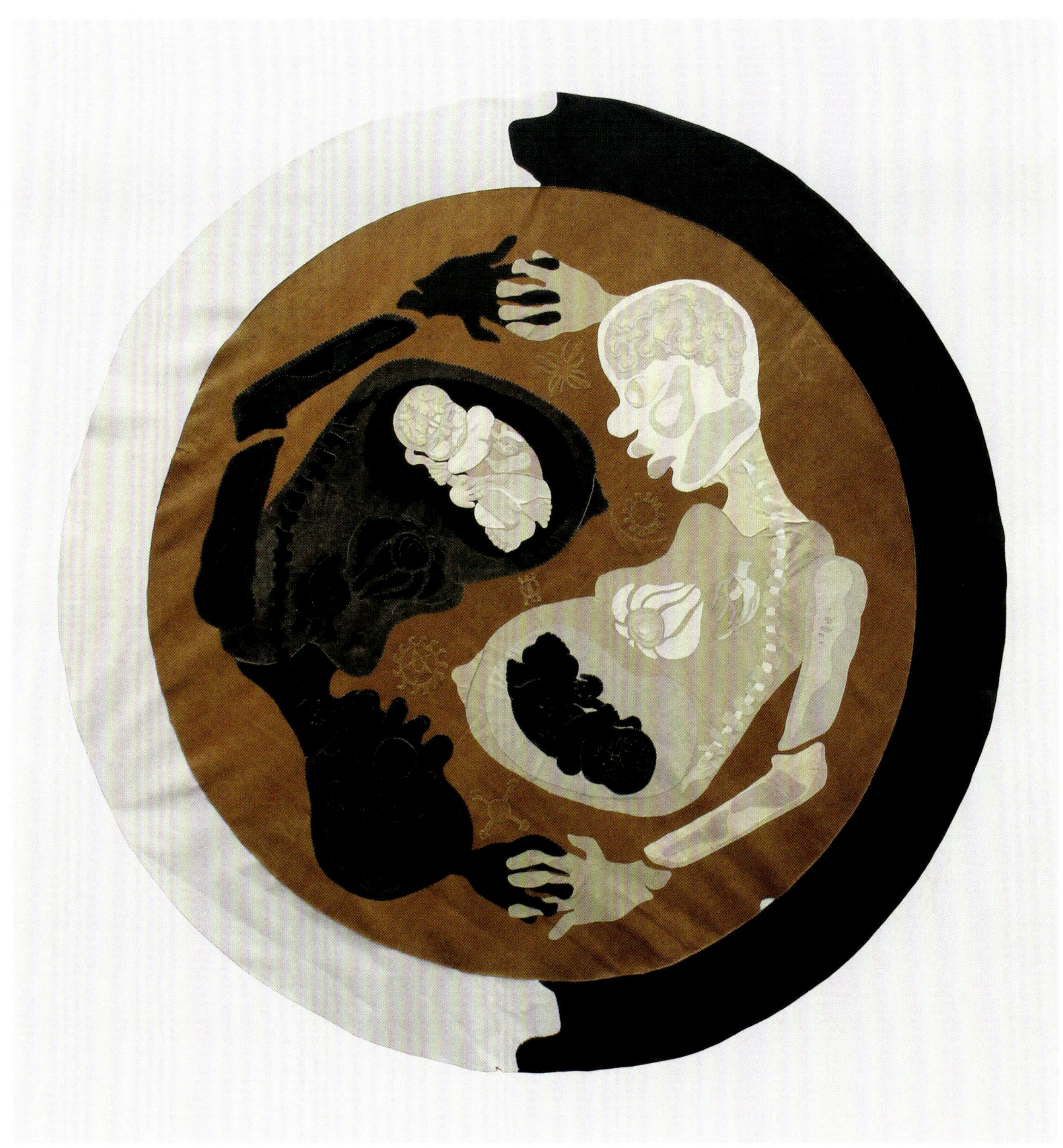

Opposite: *Knot of Pacification*, 2021. Recycled leather, wool, and suede. 114 × 100 inches (289.6 × 254 cm). Shah Garg Collection. Courtesy the artist and Night Gallery, Los Angeles

The seed of the wawa tree, 2020. Recycled leather. 59 × 59 inches (149.9 × 149.9 cm). Private collection. Courtesy the artist and Night Gallery, Los Angeles

One of Lewis's most personal works, the soft portrait *Untitled (play dumb to catch wise)* (2017), affectionately known as Lil' Gal, evokes the artist herself. Lil' Gal's plaster face is reminiscent of Lewis's, her hair is constituted of the artist's own locks, and she wears a hat and fragments of clothing formerly worn by the artist. Most of the time, Lil' Gal lives in Lewis's studio or with her at home, but when presented in exhibitions, she lounges on a colorful rocking chair, often surrounded by stuffed animals. Like other of Lewis's soft portraits and assemblages, such as *Heartbeat (quiet thrum)* or *Baby bumblebee*, Lil' Gal ultimately evokes a raw sense of vulnerability, the kind associated with children and childhood. For Lewis, this comes down to how "the process of creating them is reflective of personal and historical traumas, wherein every gesture, each stitch or scratch, is part of a labor of love and a material mark toward healing (spirit conservation)."[36] It makes sense that she would keep Lil' Gal close. "They feel like children to me."[37] These soft portraits are charged objects: they are alive with the energy of previously worn found fabrics, animated through every gesture, intensely personal, yet open to a world of associations.

The monumental, multipart soft sculpture *Symphony* (2020–21), displayed spectacularly in a vaulted, interstitial space at the National Gallery of Canada in Ottawa, is a singular achievement of scale. Lewis conceives of *Symphony* as a sovereign of the T.A.U.B.I.S. designation of the universe, which stands for the Triumphant Alliance of the Ubiquitous Blossoms of Incarnate Souls. According to Lewis, T.A.U.B.I.S. is an institution working to regulate the moral compass of the universe. *Symphony* comprises two figures made of delicate, recycled, and hand-dyed fabrics, both rendered in a soft palette of pinks, peaches, beiges, and gentle yellows. A large figure called *Symphony* wearing a hoop skirt has hands outstretched in a gesture of equanimity, while a smaller figure, *Chime*, is perched just below. Falling from the ceiling in long strings that spill across a two-part, circular pedestal, are Lewis's ubiquitous blossoms of colorful, hand-stitched fabric flowers. For Lewis, "the T.A.U.B.I.S. are mutable beings. Devoid of gender, they transmute into blossoms, each one containing a soul, alive and listening."[38]

This architectural sense of scale was carried forward in gigantic masks of mythical beings inspired by Yoruba masks and the writings of Nigerian playwright Wole Soyinka. In Soyinka's creative writing, including his play *A Dance of the Forests* (1960), according to scholar Gilbert Tarka Fai, "the mask is presented as a medium through which

Untitled (play dumb to catch wise), 2017. Fabric, wire, polyester stuffing, plaster, acrylic paint, human hair, and stones. 24 × 20 × 33 inches (61 × 50.8 × 83.8 cm)

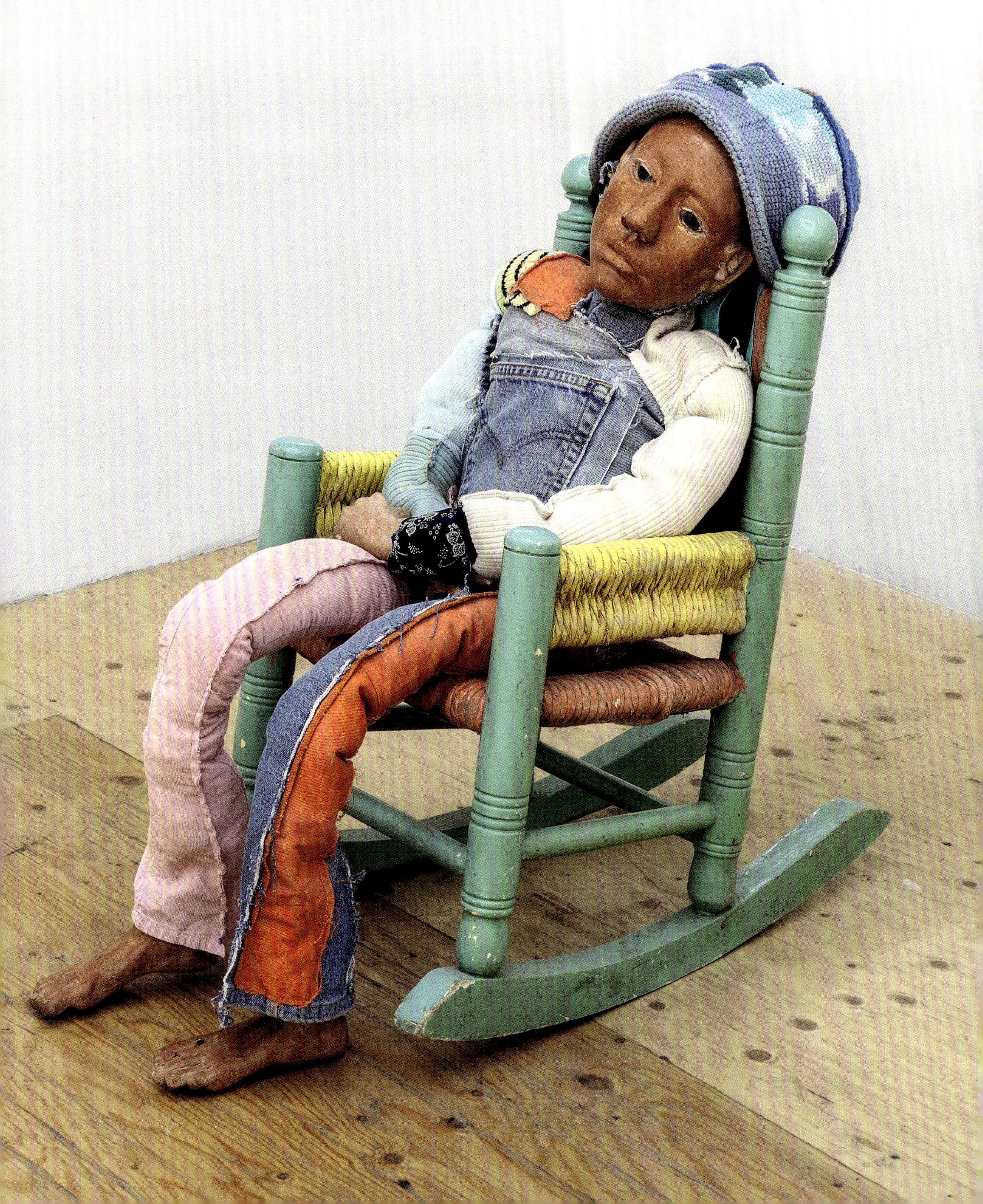

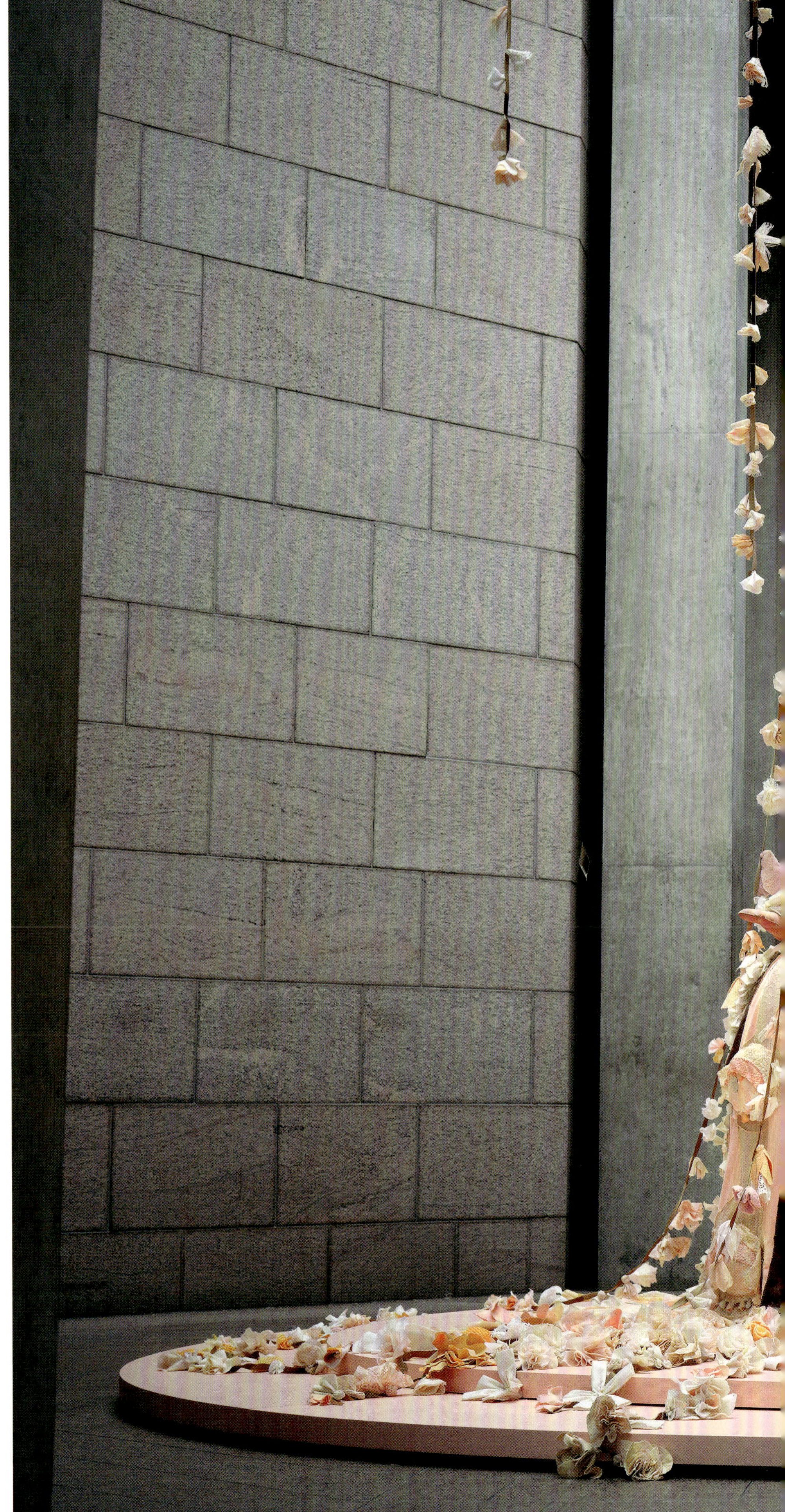

Symphony, 2019. Installation
view, *Tau Lewis: Symphony*,
National Gallery of Canada,
Ottawa, 2020–21

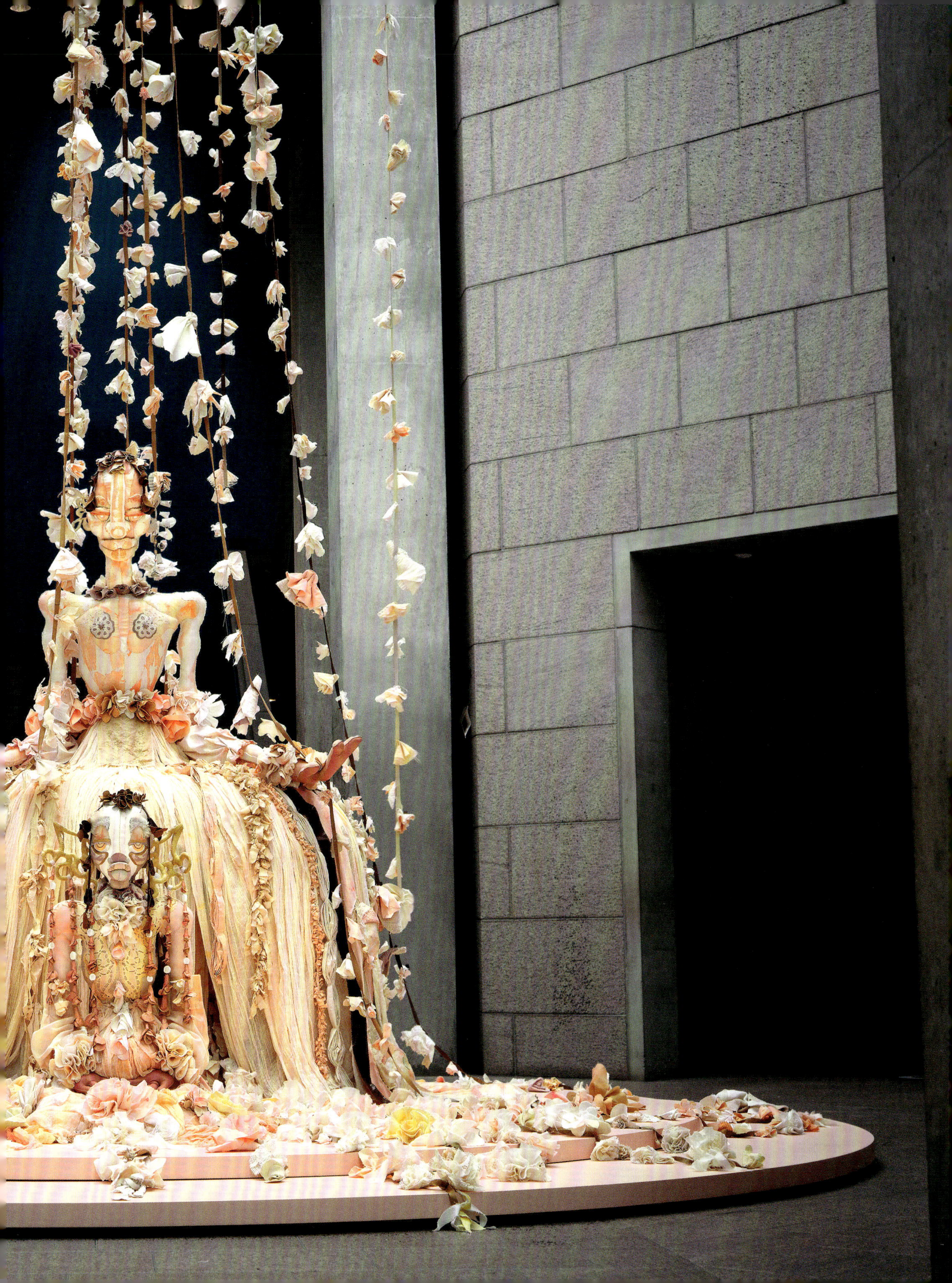

gods and spirits become manifest in the world of the living."[39] The large-scale masks made of found fabrics are often complemented by nearly identical human-scale figurative sculptures. Seen together, the masks and their complementary figurative sculptures suggest the transit between the real and spiritual worlds for gods and spirits to become manifest.

Several of these sculptures were inspired by Greek mythology. *Homonoia* (2022), for example, is the name of two sculptures inspired by the ancient Greek goddess of order and unity who is connected to the concepts of "being of one mind together" or a "union of hearts." The mask is made mostly of red, blue, brown, and beige sections of repurposed leather and suede, topped by a headpiece of five circular, antennae-like appendages. Its complement is a human-scaled reclining figure resembling a mermaid, who wears a matching headpiece. For *Saint Mozelle* (2022), a blue and green mask adorned with falling strings of blossoms like *Symphony*, Lewis was inspired by Homer's *Odyssey* and the lotus-eaters who appear in his epic poem. In Greek and Roman mythology, lotus-eaters lived on an island where they ate from the fabled lotus tree, whose narcotic fruits and flowers lulled the lotus-eaters into an unbothered indifference. Lewis sees *Saint Mozelle* as a "tutelary deity and a sanctuary," as the mask and matching figure suggest a state of calmness and protective serenity.[40]

The gigantic size of masks like *Saint Mozelle* and others like *Mater Dei* (2022), whose title is Latin for "mother of God," match in some ways the scale of the divine, godlike beings they evoke. And yet, smaller-scale soft sculptures, such as *Mutasis Moon* (2021) carry as much weight. Childlike in stature, *Mutasis Moon* is a gentle, otherworldly being with multiple faces made mostly of turquoise, white, and beige leather. *Mutasis Moon* stands tenderly with arms outstretched as if waiting for an embrace, a figure of hope and transcendence. Made from found fabric remains, it is as if this being traveled through a portal and arrived, alive and listening. It is infused with spirit, and in its presence, we remember our own smallness, our own vulnerability. In that encounter, even as we move through expansive geographies, reverberating across space and time, through the world of associations drawn together by Lewis's capacious work, we are ultimately brought into contact with ourselves. Within every work, like hidden objects, is an invitation to consider how we might conserve our own spirit, and how ideas of material transformation always relate to our own.

Homonoia, 2022. Steel, enamel paint, acrylic paint and finisher, recycled leather and suede, organic cotton twill, and coated nylon thread. 44 × 68 × 66½ inches (111.8 × 172.7 × 168.9 cm). Rennie Collection, Vancouver. Courtesy the artist and 52 Walker, New York

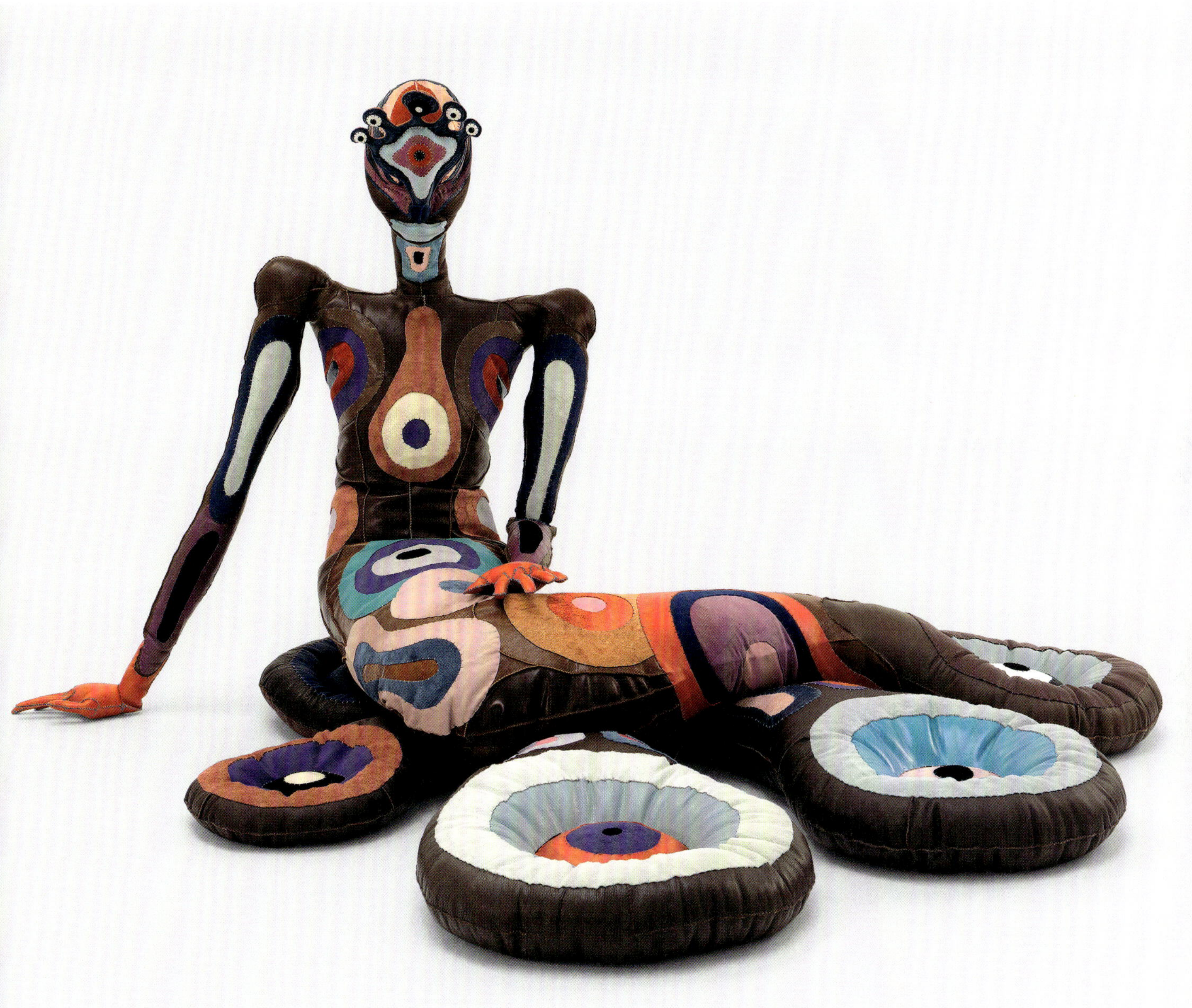

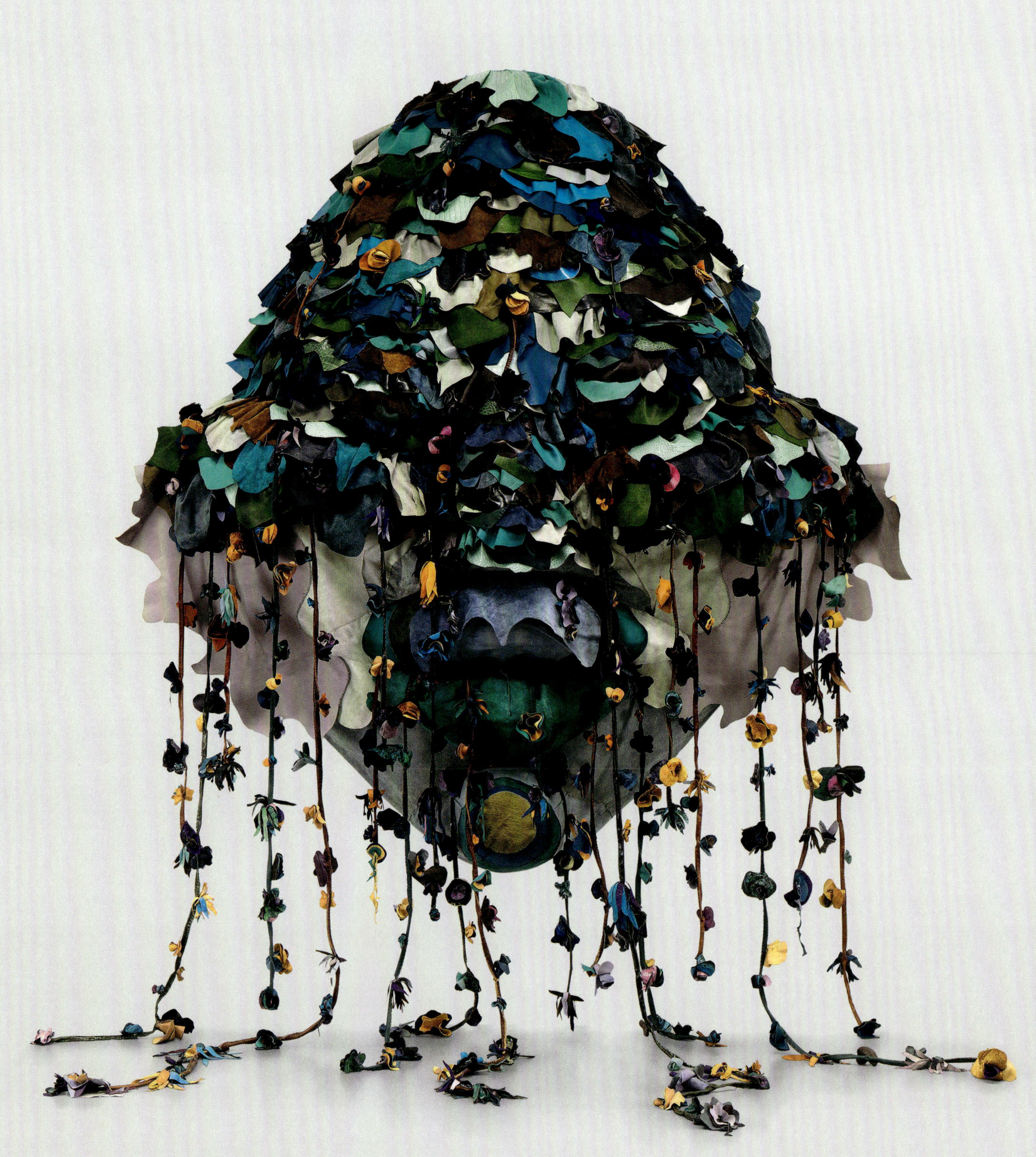

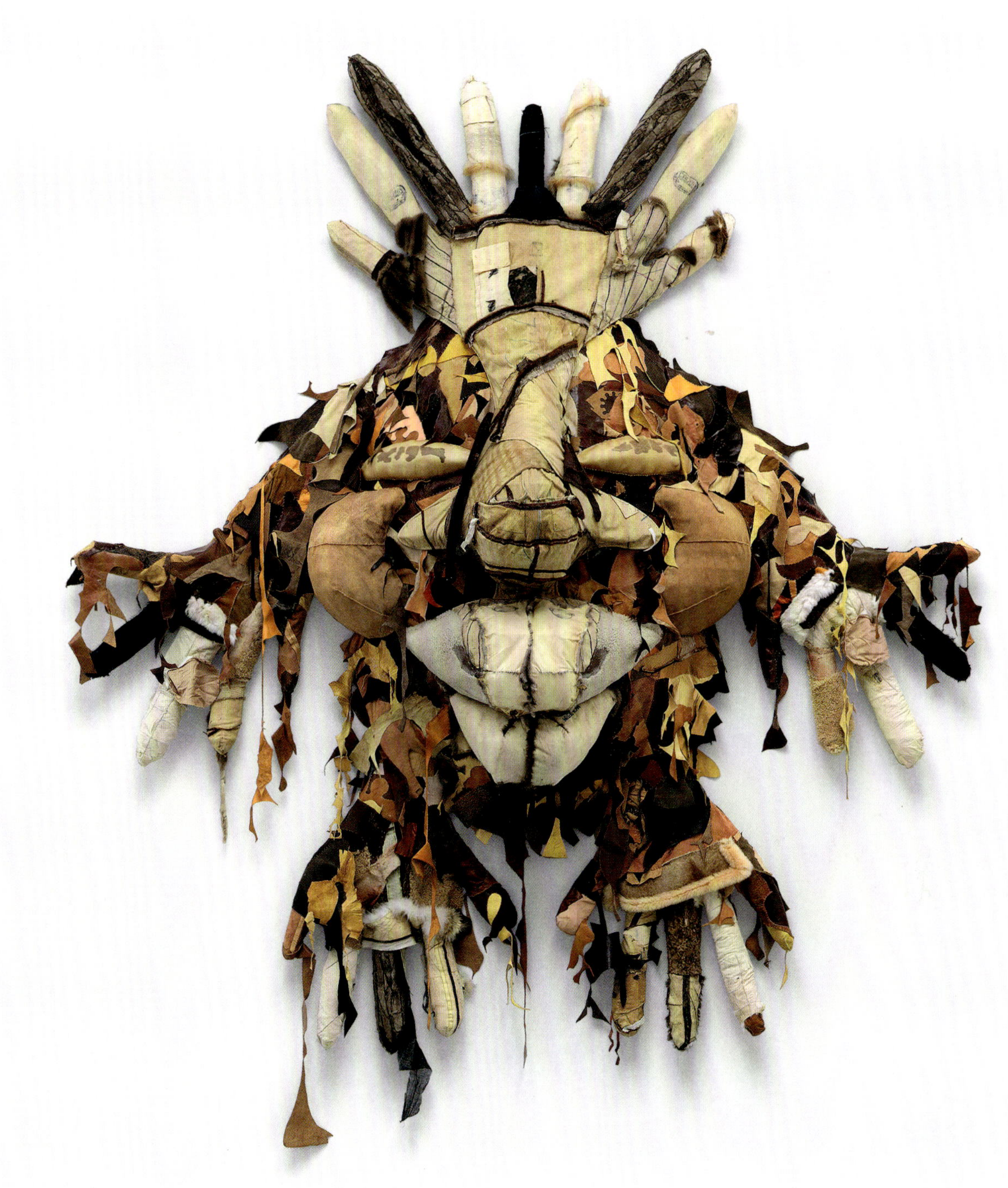

Opposite: *Saint Mozelle*, 2022. Steel, enamel paint, acrylic paint and finisher, recycled leather and suede, organic cotton twill, and coated nylon thread. 113¾ × 95¼ × 59 inches (288.9 × 241.9 × 149.9 cm). Courtesy the artist and 52 Walker, New York

Mater Dei, 2023. Steel, enamel paint, recycled leather, suede, sea glass, conch shells, pebbles, wood, organic cotton twill, and coated nylon thread. 65 × 69 × 51 inches (165.1 × 175.3 × 129.5 cm). Private collection. Courtesy the artist and 52 Walker, New York

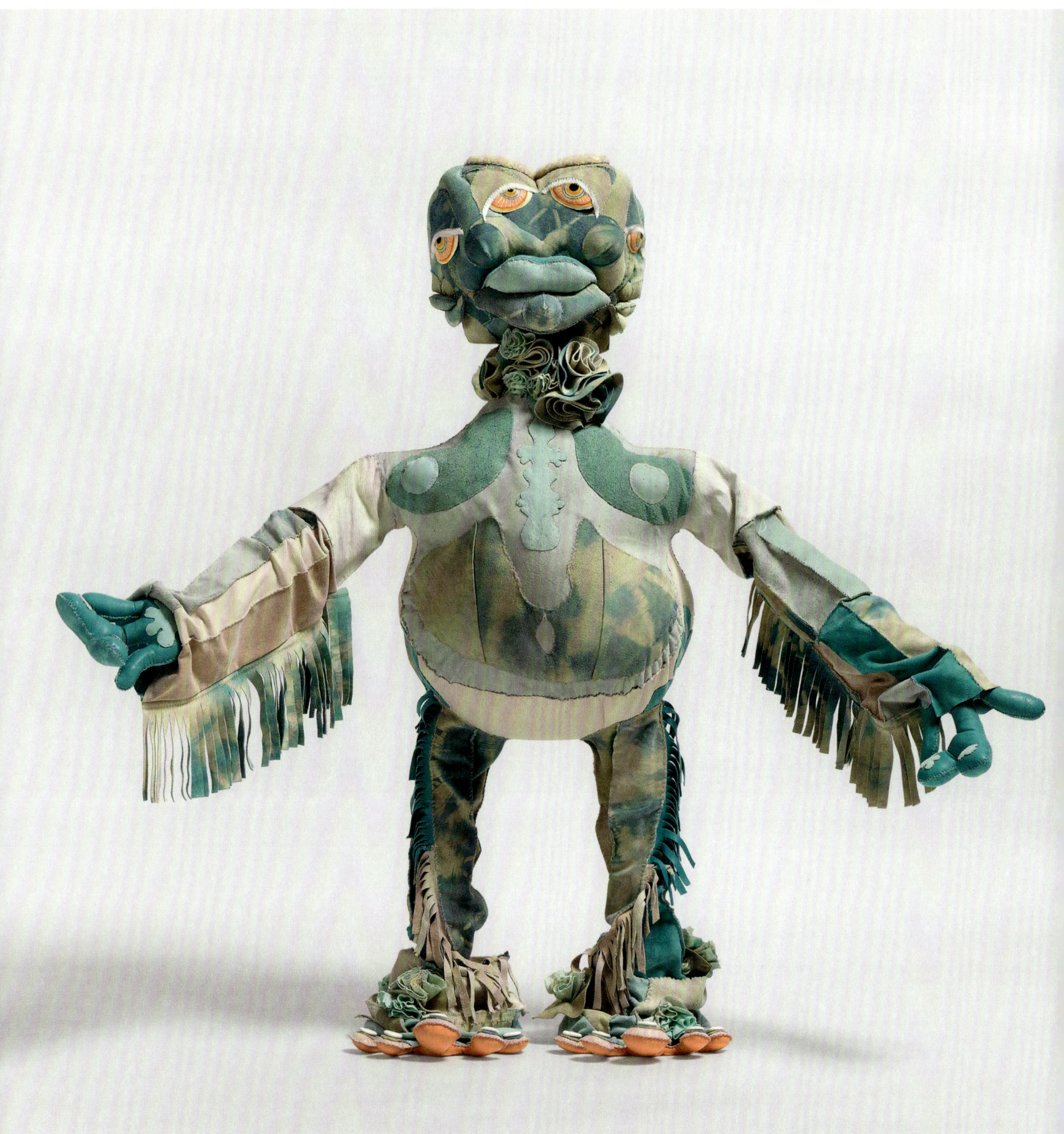

NOTES

1. National Ocean Service, "What Is a Rossby Wave?" https://oceanservice.noaa.gov
    /facts/rossby-wave.html.

2. Anthropologist Stefan Helmreich offers the phrase "Radio Ocean" to describe how
    ocean waves might be imagined as akin to radio waves. Stefan Helmreich, *A Book of
    Waves* (Durham, NC: Duke University Press, 2023), 148.

3. According to Kenneth Bilby, "few other countries have contributed as much as Jamaica
    to the technologically based reconfiguring of the global popular soundscape that
    started to gain momentum during the last few decades of the twentieth century."
    Kenneth Bilby, "From Sound Culture to Sound System Culture: Grounding Jamaica's
    Ultramodern Music in an Ancestral Livity," in *Comprendiendo/Understanding
    América*, ed. Fernando Palacios Mateos (Quito, Ecuador: Centro de Publicaciones
    PUCE), 86. For David Toop, "dub music is like a long echo delay, looping through
    time. Regenerating every few years, sometimes so quiet that only a disciple could
    hear, sometime [*sic*] shatteringly loud." David Toop, *Ocean of Sound: Aether Talk,
    Ambient Sound and Imaginary Worlds* (London: Serpent's Tail, 1995), 115.

4. Toop, *Ocean of Sound*, 115.

5. Toop, *Ocean of Sound*, 116.

6. Alexis Pauline Gumbs, *Dub: Finding Ceremony* (Durham, NC: Duke University Press,
    2020), xiii.

7. "Tau Lewis and the Landscapes of Canada," *Muse Magazine*, October 11, 2018,
    https://agnes.queensu.ca/connect/news-and-stories/tau-lewis-and-the-landscapes
    -of-canada/.

8. Paul Gilroy, *The Black Atlantic: Modernity and Double Consciousness* (New York:
    Verso, 1993), 32. According to Lewis: "music is a huge part of my life too, I can't exist
    without it, I can't work without it, I can't dream without it." For many years, Lewis's
    father ran a dub club in Toronto that featured a traditional Jamaican sound system.

9. Tau Lewis, with commentary by Jack Levinson, "Tau Lewis: Celestial Bodies and the
    Moral Compass of the Universe," *National Gallery of Canada Magazine*, July 27, 2021,
    https://www.gallery.ca/magazine/exhibitions/tau-lewis-celestial-bodies-and-the
    -moral-compass-of-the-universe.

10. Liner notes for *The Quest* (Submerge, 1997).

11. Kodwo Eshun, "Further Considerations on Afrofuturism," *CR* 3, no. 2 (2003): 300,
    https://dx.doi.org/10.1353/ncr.2003.0021.

12. Eshun, "Further Considerations on Afrofuturism," 300.

13. DeForrest Brown Jr., *Assembling a Black Counter Culture* (New York: Primary Informa-
    tion, 2022), 347.

14. Brown, *Assembling a Black Counter Culture*, 323.

15. Tau Lewis, in conversation with the author, January 13, 2024.

16. Gumbs, *Dub*, xii.

17. Gumbs, *Dub*.

18. Tau Lewis in conversation with Charlotte Jansen, "The Artist Making Low-Cost and
    Eco-Friendly Sculptures," *Elephant*, July 1, 2019, https://elephant.art/artist-making
    -low-cost-eco-friendly-sculptures/.

19. Magdalyn Asimakis, "Material Frequencies: The Sculptural Work of Tau Lewis,"
    https://kagcag.usask.ca/images/2019/tau-lewis-essay.pdf.

20. Lewis and Levinson, "Tau Lewis."

21. Lewis and Levinson, "Tau Lewis."

22. Lewis, quoted in "Tau Lewis × 52 Walker: *See the True Work of Angels*," David Zwirner,
    https://www.davidzwirner.com/viewing-room/2023/tau-lewis-x-52-walker-see-the
    -true-work-of-angels.

Mutasis Moon, 2021. Recycled leather, seashells, sand dollars, acrylic paint, PVC pipe, galvanized steel, muslin, and recycled polyester fibers. 40 × 41½ × 15 inches (101.6 × 105.5 × 38 cm). Courtesy the artist and Sadie Coles HQ, London. Private collection

23. Linda Goode Bryant and Marcy S. Philips, preface to *Contextures* (New York: Just Above Midtown, 1978), 9.

24. Goode Bryant and Philips, *Contextures*, 39–40.

25. Goode Bryant and Philips, *Contextures*, 40.

26. David Hammons in conversation with Kellie Jones, "Interview: David Hammons," *Art Papers* (July/August, 1988).

27. From Betye Saar's 1980 text on ritual, reproduced in *Betye Saar: Ritual* (Culver City, CA: Roberts and Tilton, 2016), https://issuu.com/robertsprojects/docs/betyesaarritual_copy.

28. Lonnie Holley, quoted in Judith McWillie, "Lonnie Holley's Moves," *Artforum* 30, no. 8 (April 1992), https://www.artforum.com/features/lonnie-holleys-moves-203567/.

29. Katherine McKittrick, "Keeping the Heartbreak," in *Don't Wear Down: Essays and Ideas* (2019), 25, https://katherinemckittrick.com/wornout/. Accessed October 17, 2019. This piece is no longer posted online. It can be accessed by contacting the author.

30. "Everything is a time capsule" is the title of a book Lewis published by Magenta Foundation in 2017.

31. Lewis, in conversation with the author, January 17, 2024.

32. Joanne Cubbs, "*Freedom Cloth*," Souls Grown Deep, https://www.soulsgrowndeep.org/artist/thornton-dial/work/freedom-cloth.

33. Lewis, quoted in Julia Halperin, "Fiber Art Is Finally Being Taken Seriously," *New York Times Style Magazine*, September 11, 2023, https://www.nytimes.com/2023/09/11/t-magazine/fiber-art-textiles.html.

34. Adinkra Symbols and Meanings: Explore African Symbols and Meanings, https://www.adinkrasymbols.org/.

35. Max Kozloff, "The Poetics of Softness," in *Renderings: Critical Essays on a Century of Modern Art* (New York: Simon and Schuster, 1968), 224.

36. Lewis, quoted in Tiana Reid "Tau Lewis's 'Secret Objects,'" Topical Cream, June 18, 2018, https://topicalcream.org/features/tau-lewiss-secret-objects/.

37. Lewis, quoted in Reid "Tau Lewis's 'Secret Objects.'"

38. Lewis and Levinson, "Tau Lewis."

39. Gilbert Tarka Fai, "Soyinka and Yoruba Sculpture: Masks of Deification and Symbolism," *Rupkatha Journal on Interdisciplinary Studies in Humanities* 2, no. 1 (2010): 45, https://dx.doi.org/10.21659/rupkatha.v2n1.05, and http://rupkatha.com/V2/n1/SoyinkaandYorubaSculpture.pdf.

40. Lewis, quoted in "Tau Lewis × 52 Walker."

Vena Cava, 2021. Steel, recycled leather, acrylic paint, and coated nylon thread. 121½ × 84 × 43 inches (308.6 × 213.4 × 109.2 cm). Tia Collection, Santa Fe

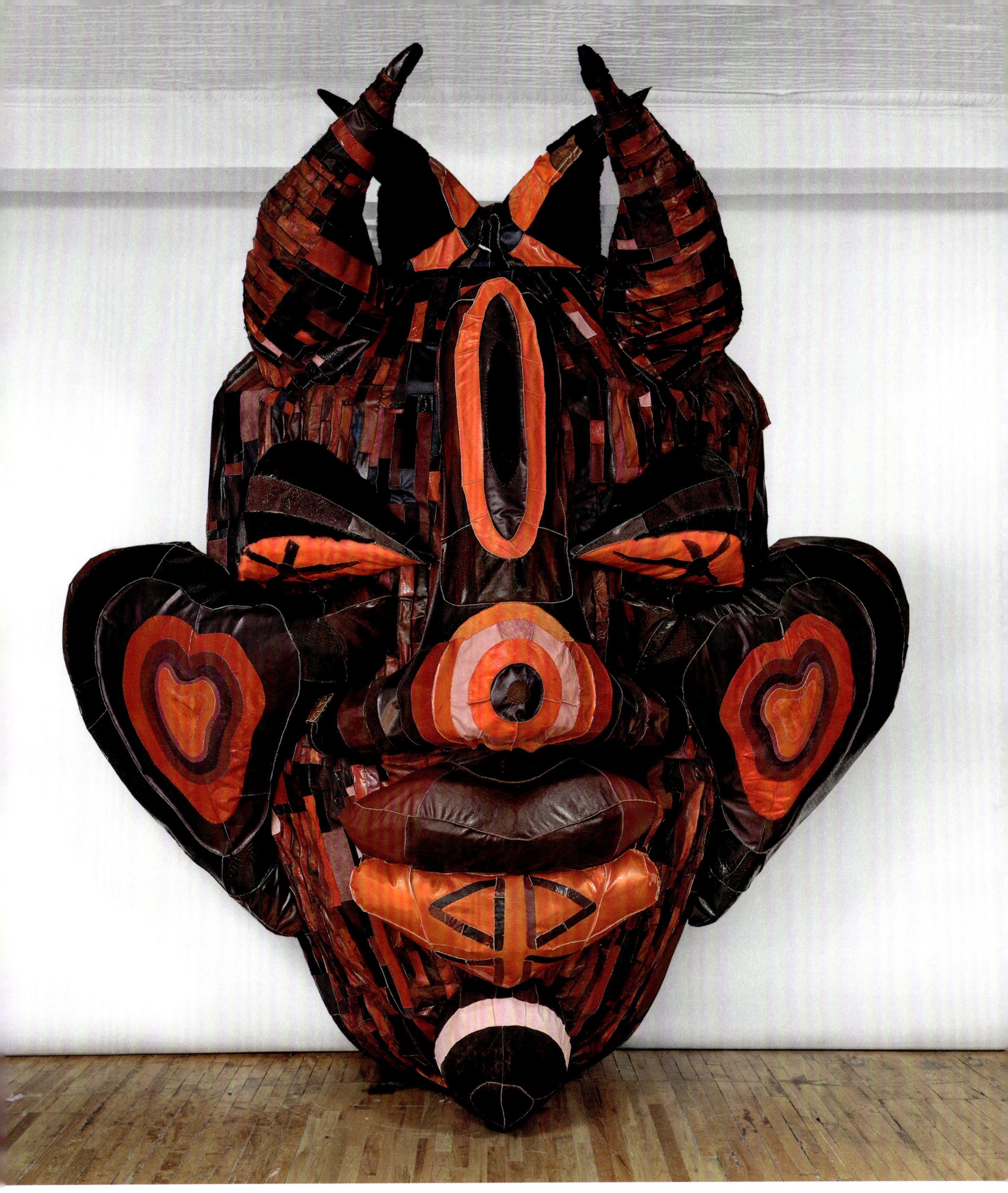

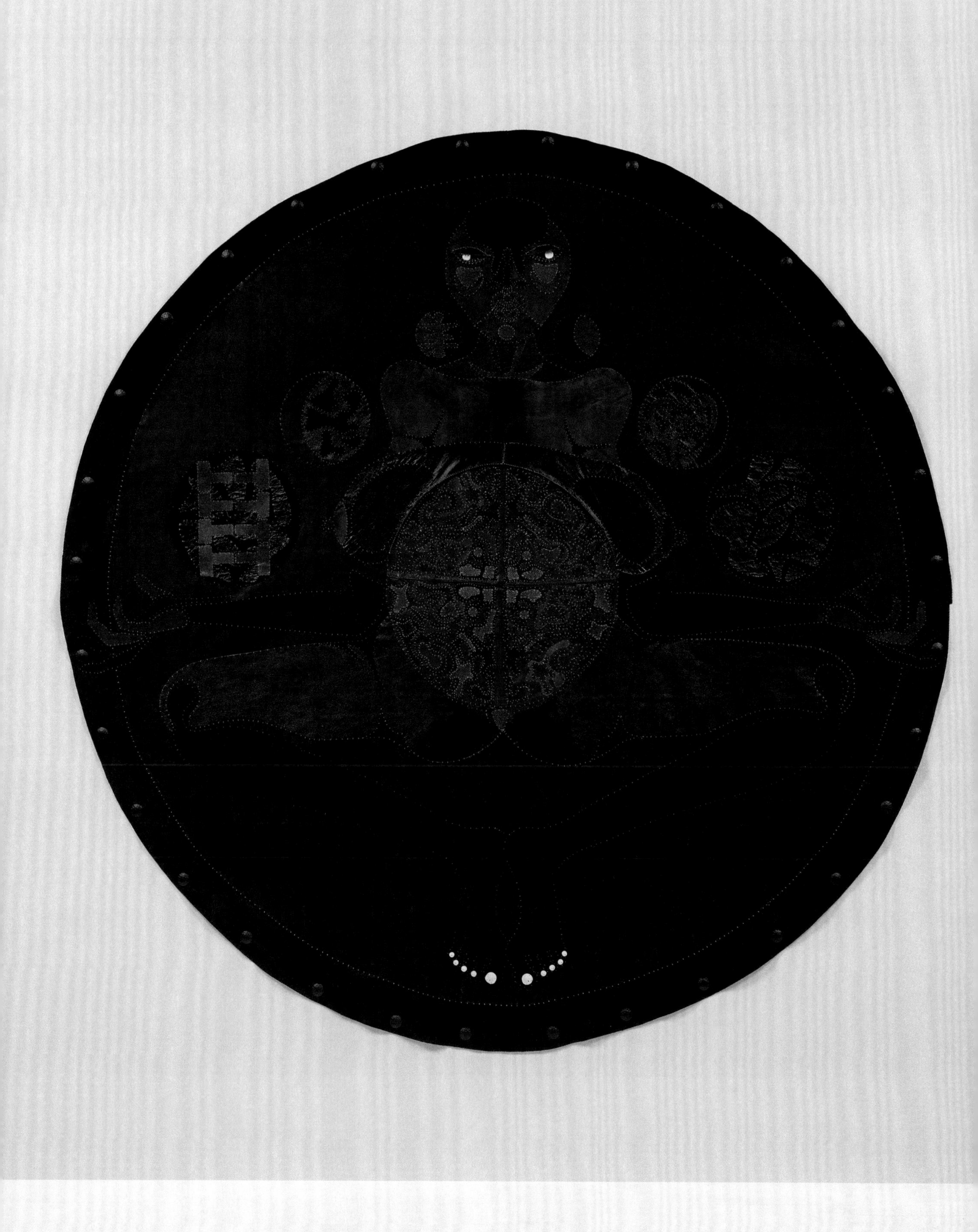

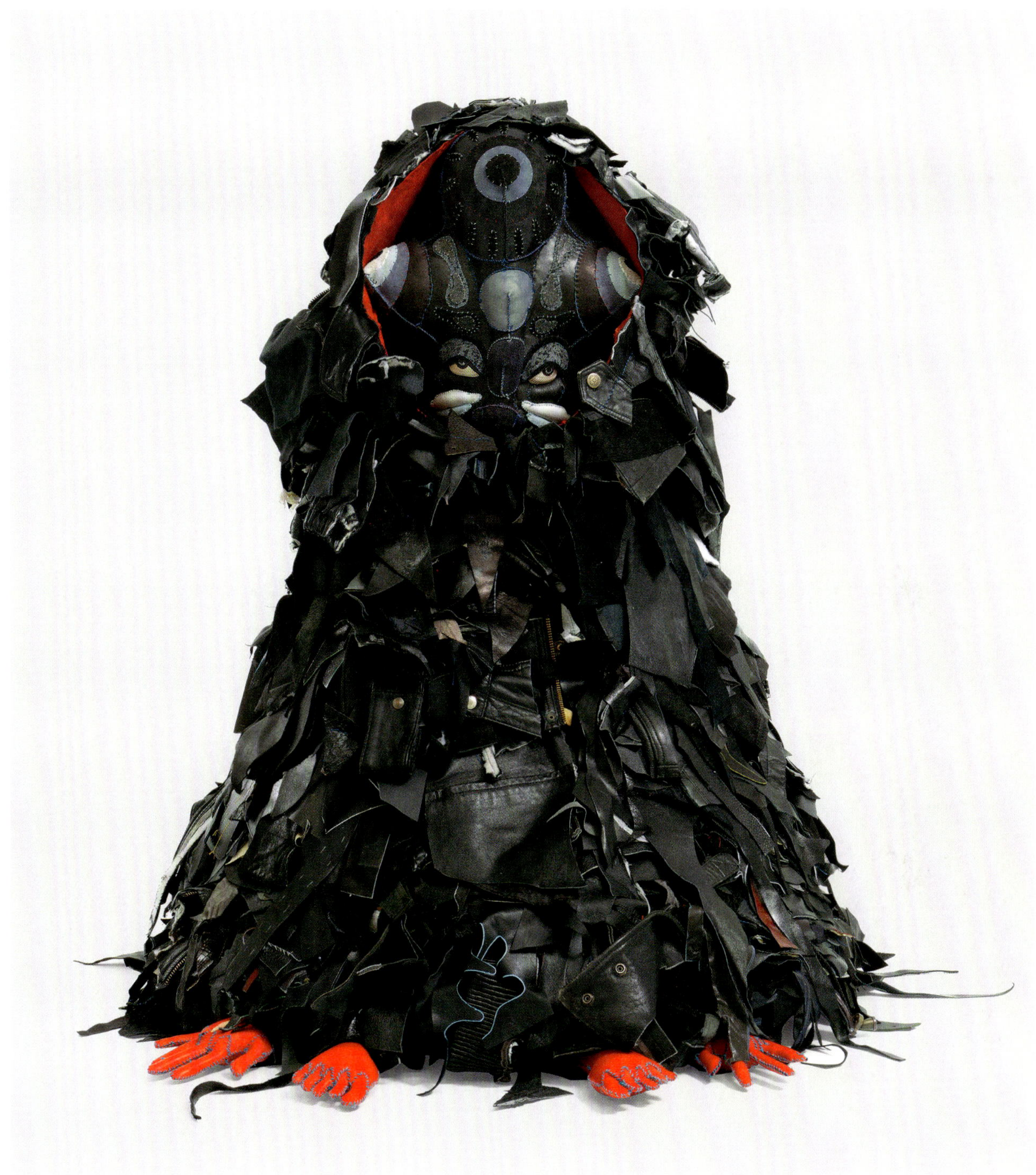

Opposite: *The talons of the eagle, the ladder of death, by God's grace, all will be well*, 2021. New and recycled leathers, stingray shagreen, and sand dollars. 86 × 86 inches (218.4 × 218.4 cm). Private collection

Trident, 2022. Steel, enamel paint, acrylic paint and finisher, recycled leather, fur, suede, shearling, shagreen, snake skin, clam shells, organic cotton twill, and coated nylon thread. 39¼ × 44 × 36 inches (99.7 × 111.8 × 91.4 cm). Private collection

Overleaf: *Return of the Martian Water God* (detail), 2022. Recycled leather, vinyl, suede, acrylic paint, leather primer, PVA glue, leather cement, cattle bone bead, Dutch trading bead, wooden dowel, and steel bracket. 68 × 110 × 10 inches (172.7 × 279.4 × 25.4 cm). Gochman Family Collection

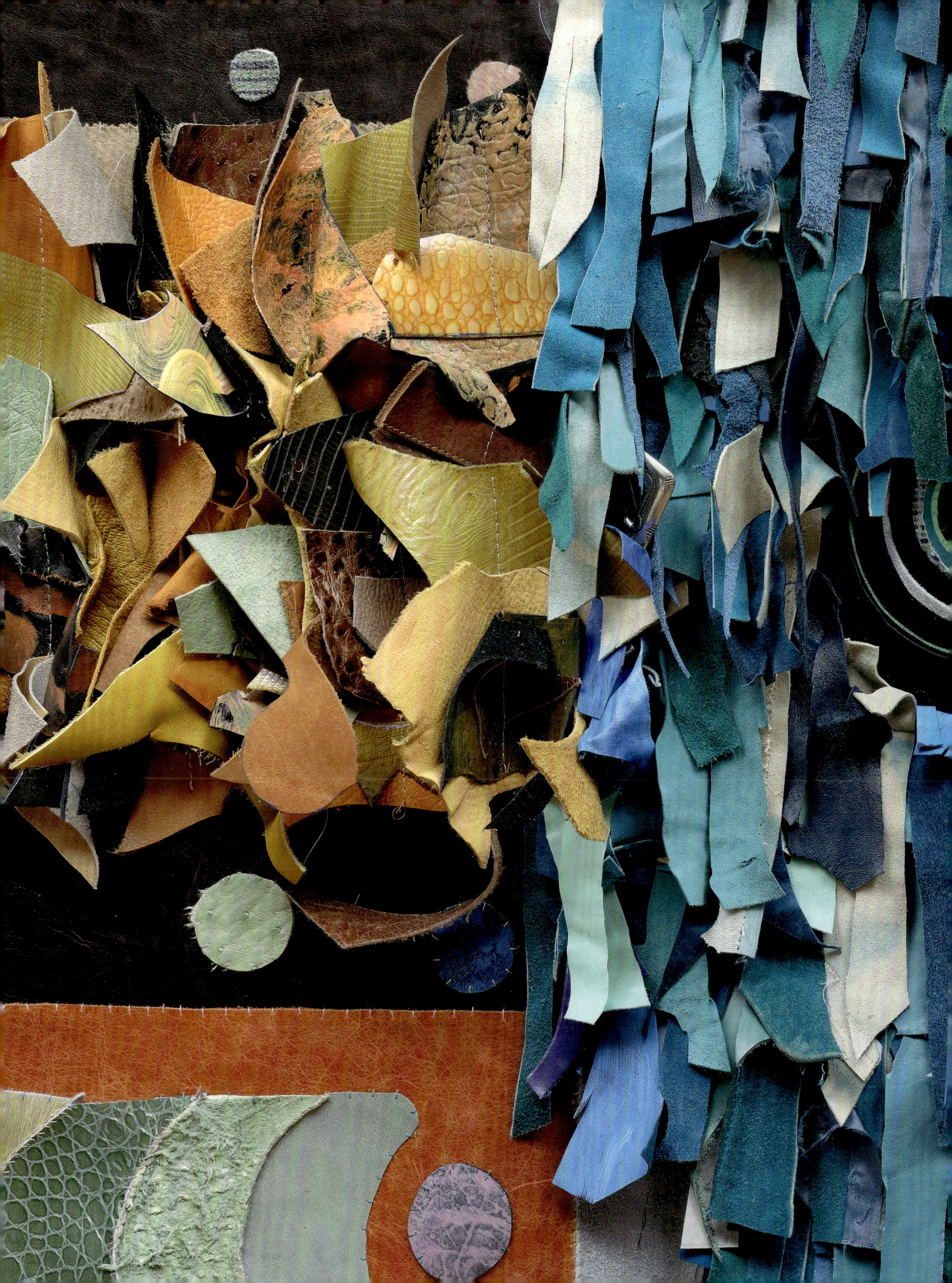

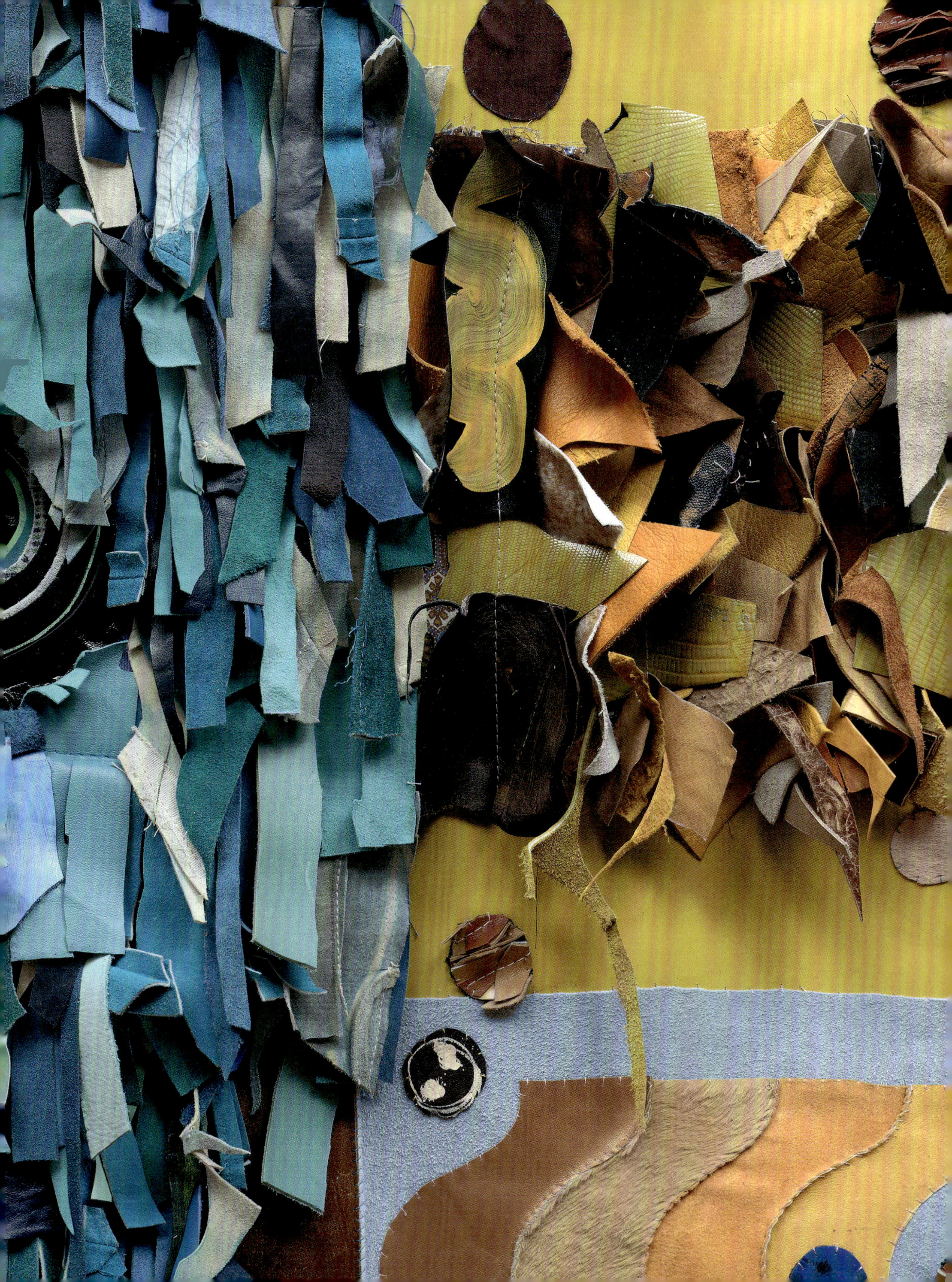

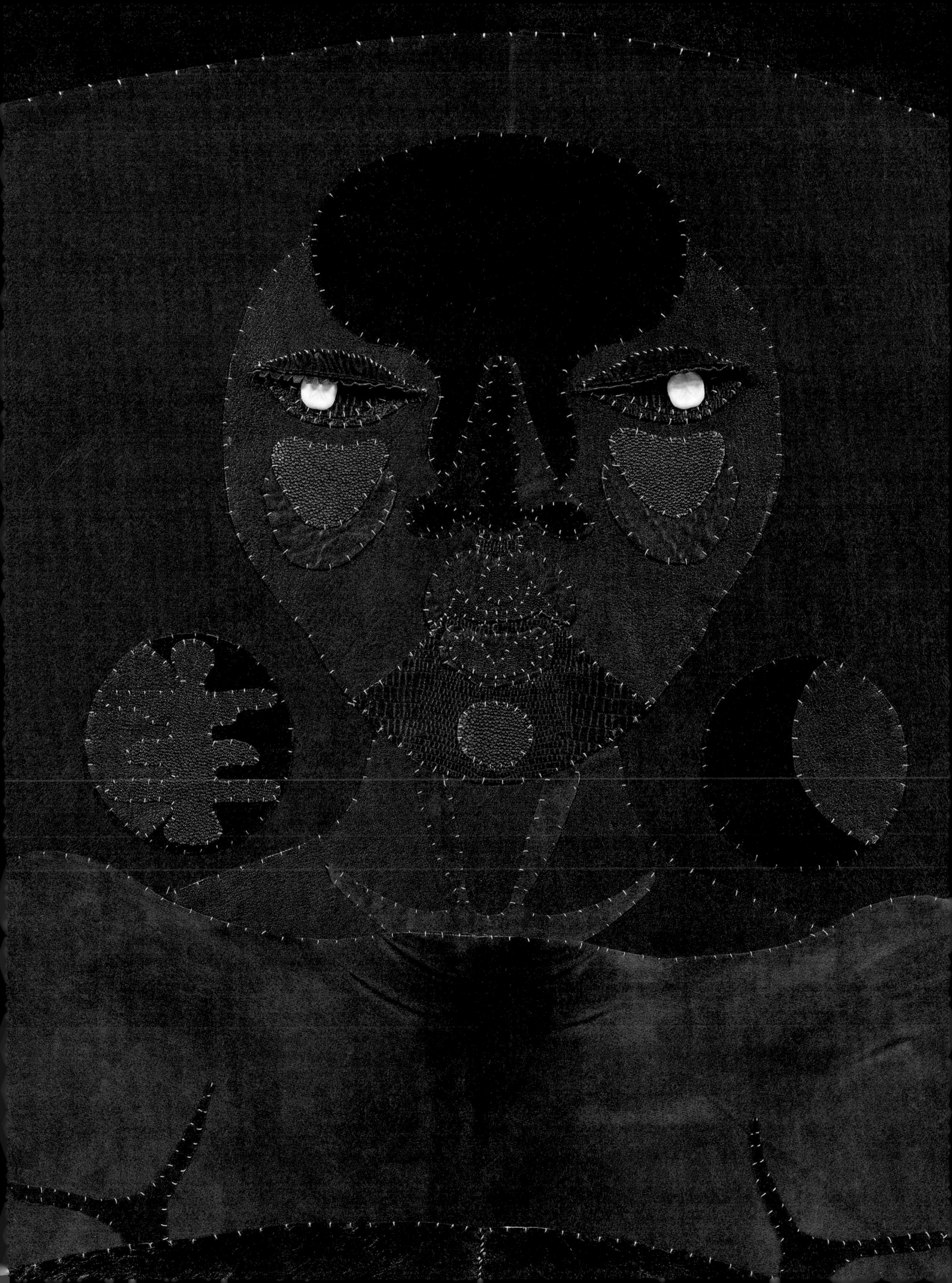

Lonnie Holley and Tau Lewis

MODERATED BY

Jeffrey De Blois

The talons of the eagle, the ladder of death, by God's grace, all will be well (detail), 2021. New and recycled leathers, stingray shagreen, and sand dollars. 86 × 86 inches (218.4 × 218.4 cm). Private collection

Jeffrey De Blois How and why did you two first connect, and how did you understand that there was a kind of sympathetic vibration between you two?

Tau Lewis I had an inspiration wall in my studio where I would pin photos and clippings and memorabilia, as well as a pad to jot down any names that came up in conversation during studio visits. Visitors would sometimes reference artists, whose names I would write down to look up later. That's been part of my education. If someone's work resonates with me, I make an effort to see it in person, or hopefully, if that artist is still alive, I try to find a way to meet them in person. I had a breakthrough when I saw images of Lonnie's work. I was twenty-two, and was working so intuitively and with such urgency, that I had very little knowledge of my forerunners. With Lonnie, I sort of felt like I'd found my person. We're speaking the same language, and I'm just learning to speak. It struck a chord in my heart and really confirmed for me that I have to keep doing what I'm doing even though it's hard on me sometimes. I still feel this gut-wrenching feeling when I hear Lonnie sing and

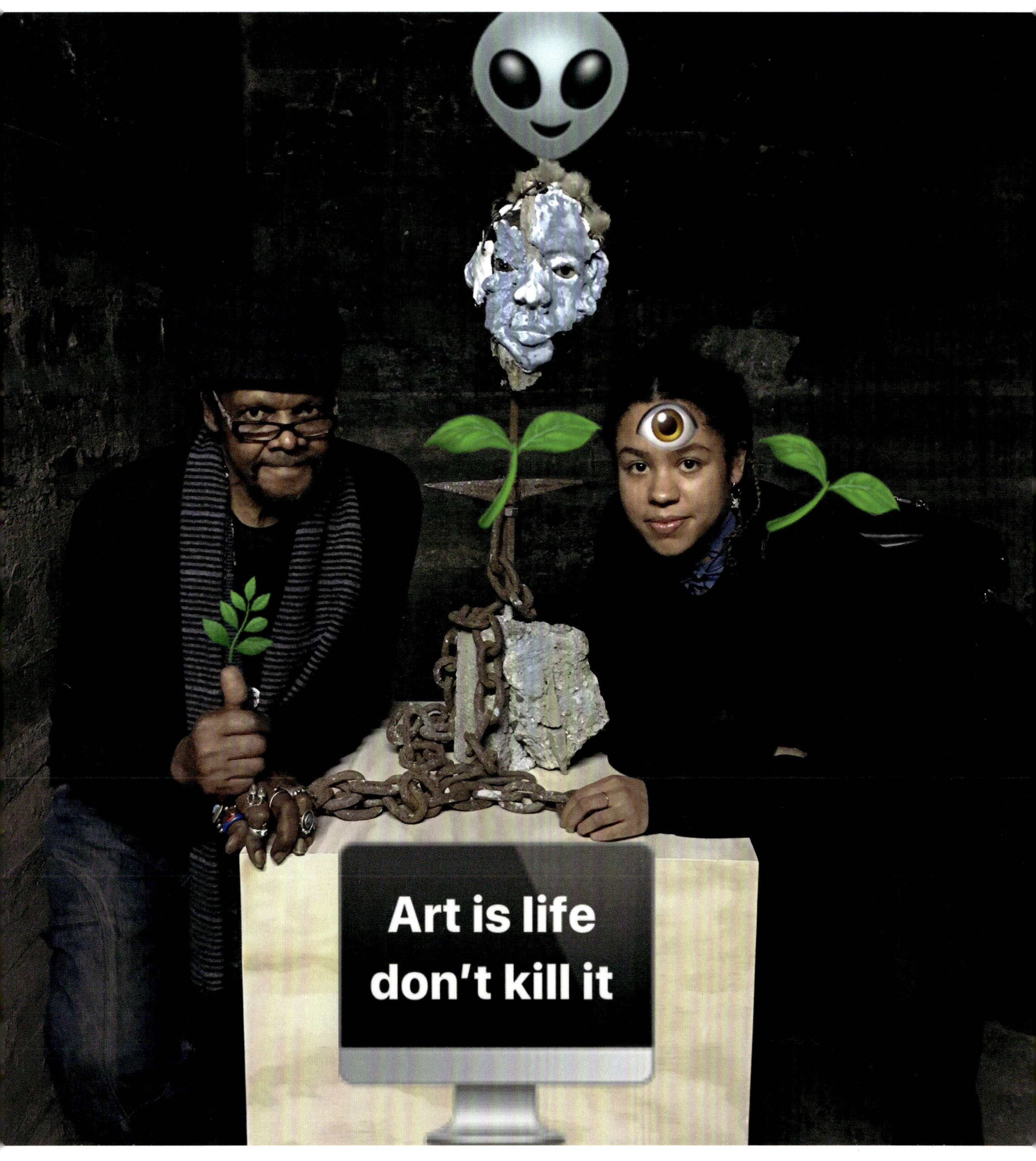
Art is life
don't kill it

when I see Lonnie's work. I started mapping out a plan to find him in Atlanta. A few months after setting that intention, it was confirmed that I would have an exhibition at Atlanta Contemporary. I was excited and nervous about the idea that they might help me reach out to Lonnie. Joe Minter (who is another one of my artistic heroes I had learned about after finding Lonnie's work), was opening an exhibition in the main gallery at Atlanta Contemporary at the same time as me. I arrived to the opening and my heart was pounding. The curator, Daniel Fuller, led me down into my show, and Lonnie was just there beside one of my sculptures. He was interpreting my sculpture for another gallery visitor. When I approached him, he clasped my hands and looked at me very intensely, and then he started to guide me through the details of my sculpture. I remember holding myself back from crying at first, and then feeling very present in that moment.

Lonnie Holley   We don't all claim to be making sacrifices to our ancestors, but in a sense, that's what I felt about her works. I saw her as more like an angelic person. I don't know how to give her a title, but I know that she's serving a spiritual purpose. Now she is there tearing things to pieces, just tearing them to pieces, putting them back together, looking at them in a different format than they would ever be looked at. And rags—it's not from rags to riches, but just from rags to rags. I've been around a lot of the women that work with fabrics and they was more like the Gee's Bend quilters, but I hadn't see that many African American, Black, Colored, or Negroes, that was allowed the capability of showing what these fabrics and clothing meant. I just went wild about it because I know if she had accomplished that much with the fabrics of today. . . . And it brought me back to fabrics all the way back off into Africa itself. Because we had been working with fabrics, all kinds of ties and binds of material, things that were a part of our services to this mothershiply manner.

TL   Every time Lonnie gives me advice or notes about my work, it's always very specific. I think it's because he has telepathic abilities. It's weird and also affirming to be seen, and I think he is looking for solutions and has detailed visions. There is a specific sculpture he told me to make once of a lamb. I haven't made it yet, but I still think that I will. He commented on my use of chains and heavy metal and told me I'd be needing a break from those materials. He told me that piecing together metal, shells, hair, and things like that will break my heart.

Lonnie Holley and Tau Lewis, untitled digital collage, 2018

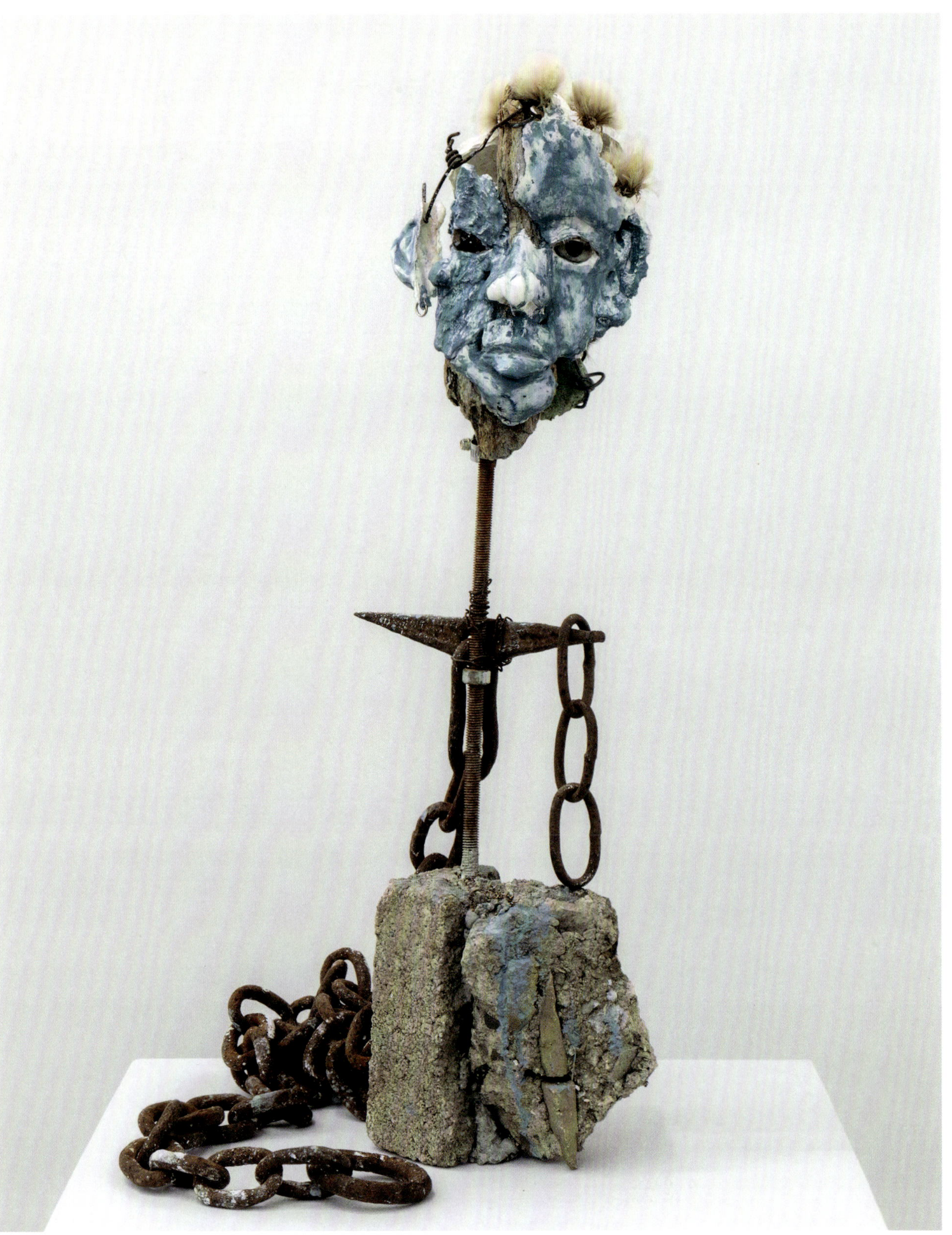

Opposite: *Big tooth (angels
in a sleepy current)*, 2017.
Hand-carved plaster,
stones, wire, acrylic paint,
fur, milk thistle seeds,
earring, driftwood, rebar,
chain, and concrete.
Dimensions unknown.
Private collection

Seashell (grinner), 2017.
Hand-carved plaster, wire,
acrylic paint, stones, reef
stones, fur, chain, paint can,
rebar, concrete, earring,
and seashell. 25½ × 13 ×
16 inches (64.8 × 33 ×
40.6 cm). Private collection

Overleaf: *Big tooth (angels
in a sleepy current* (detail),
2017

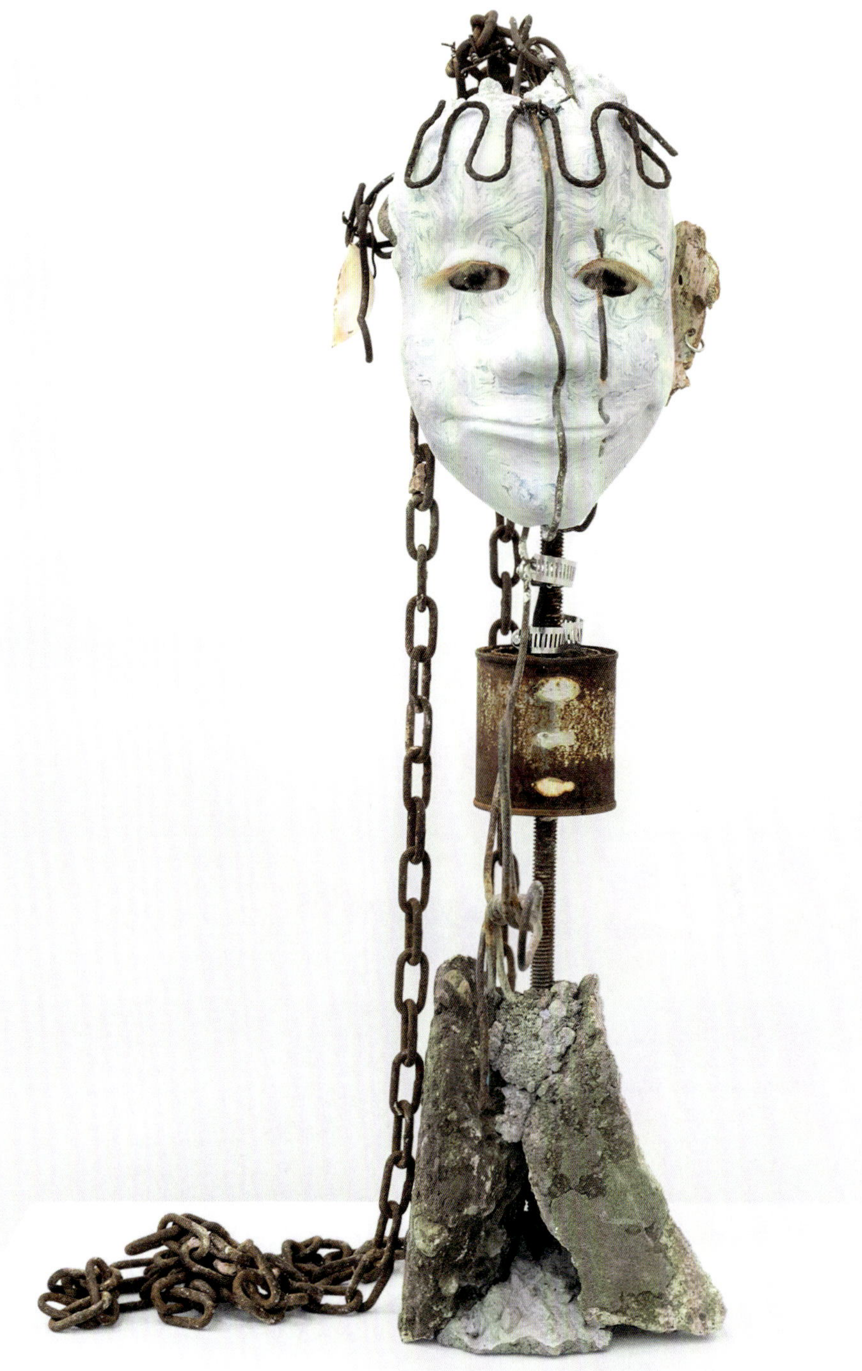

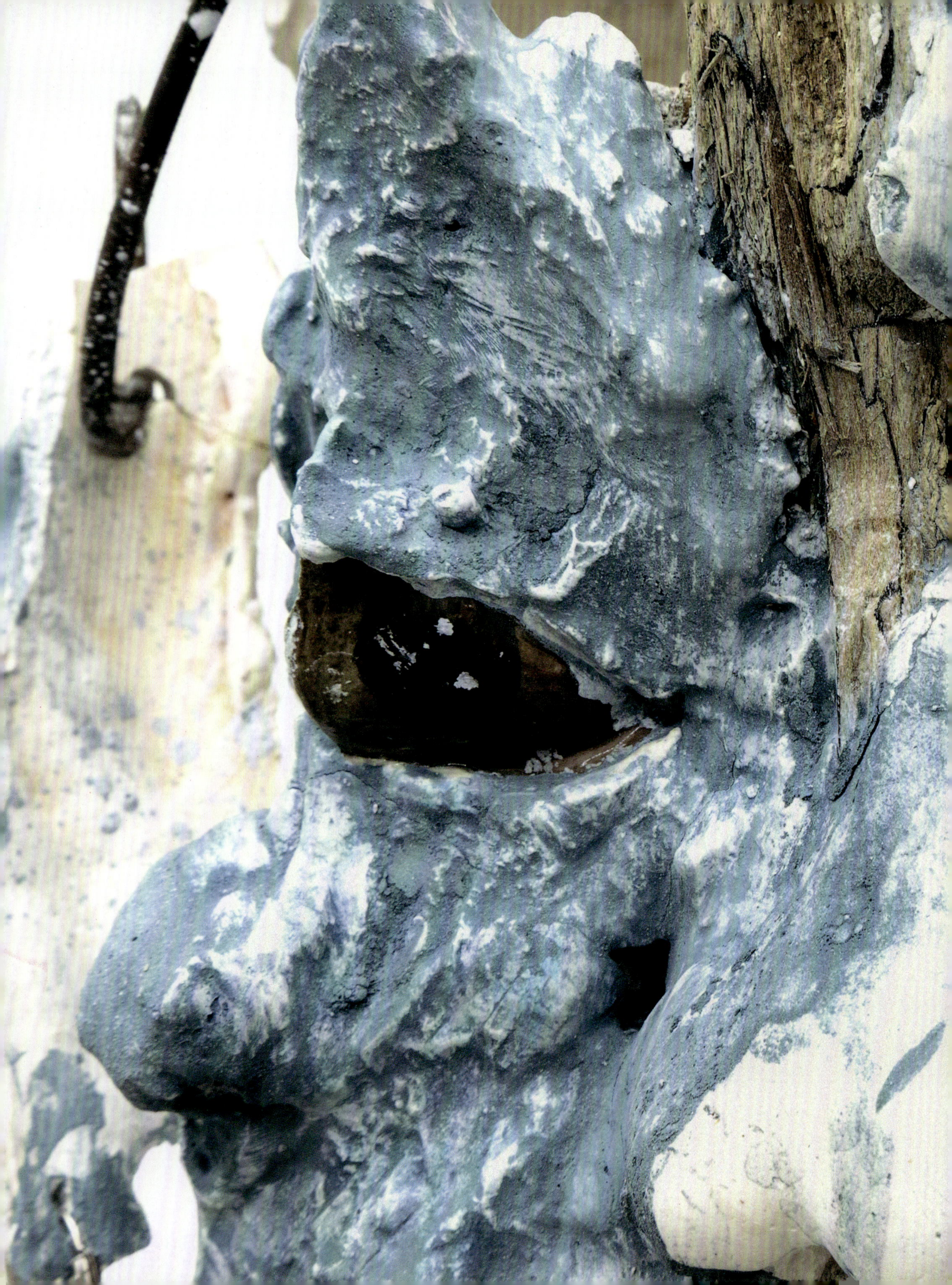

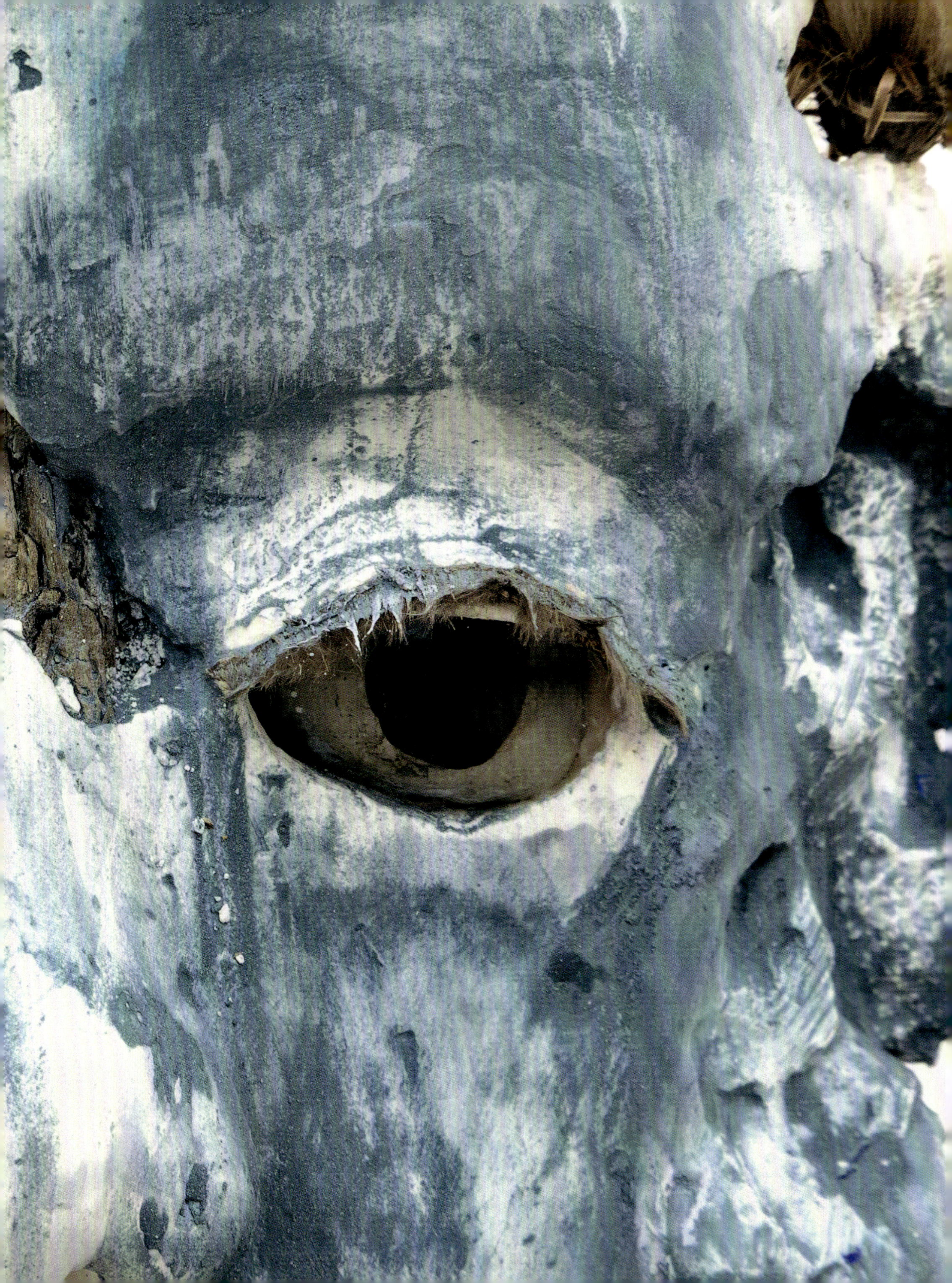

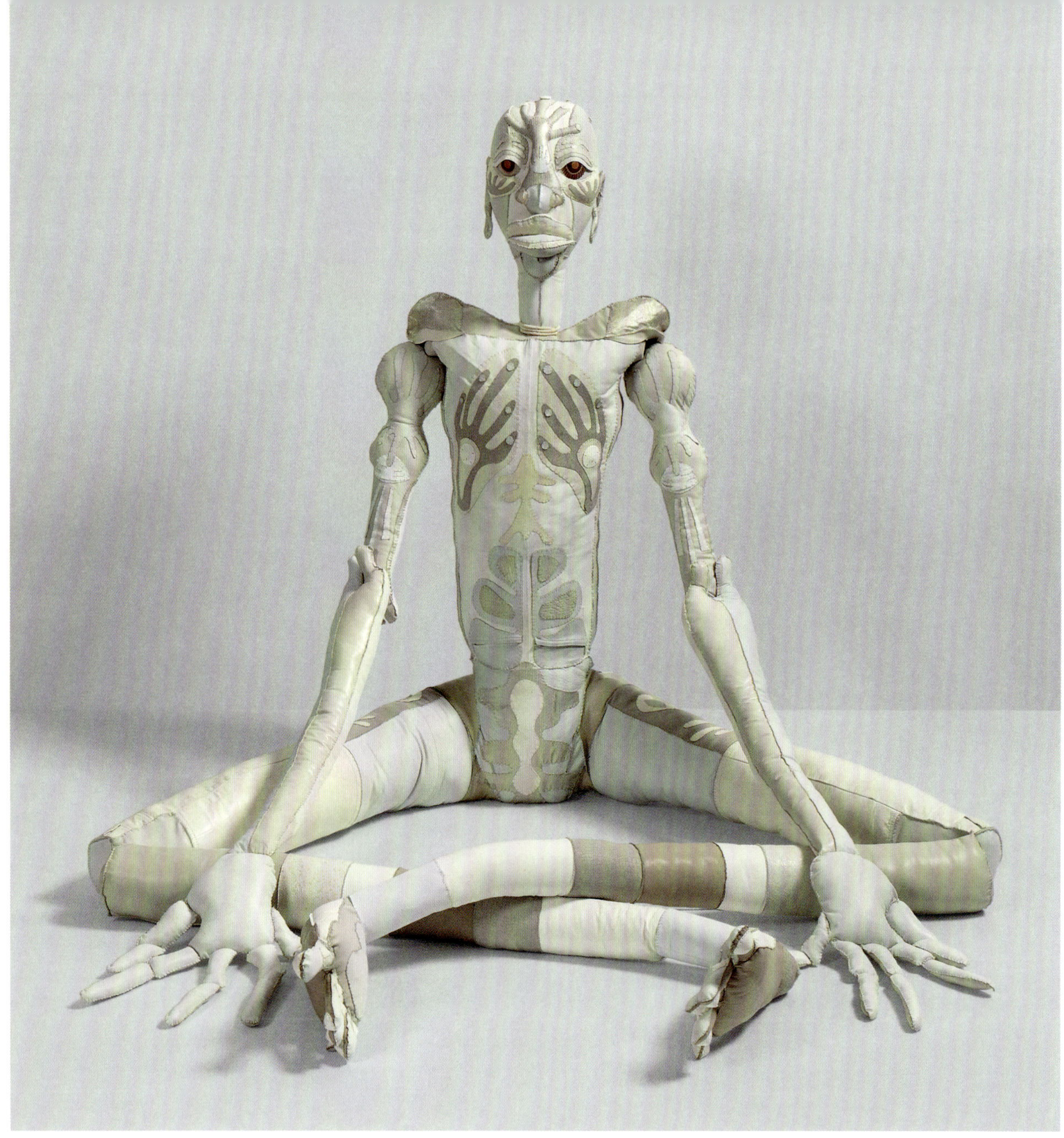

Dumah, 2021. Recycled leather, recycled polyester fibers, sand dollars, acrylic paint, PVC pipe, wire, crinoid fossils, and sea-shells. 52 × 58 × 64 inches (132.1 × 147.3 × 162.6 cm). Tia Collection, Santa Fe

He'd had a broken heart because of it, and he was right, and I understand now. He encouraged my move toward fabric. It is historically a women's medium and we're also thinking about the legacy of Gee's Bend. But he urged me toward it and said I should really rip it up, and keep my feelings in it, and make it mine.

LH Just be free at it. I mean, I wanted her to get free at it, they call it freestyle. A lot of people be copying off of other people's style. I wanted

her to create her own style. I wanted her to travel and look. I wanted
her to see the transition of our brains. These things, these things have
to be taught to have a meaningful place in our lives after our ancestors
have died and passed away. When I met Tau, it was like I had met a
new sister that had made her way to freedom. I'm trying to still get to
freedom in America. I have a hard time being the artist that I am. I have
a hard time telling nothing but the truth.

JD   Both of your works are oriented to forms of movement, transformation,
and patterns of reuse that you seem naturally inclined to do, even as
you come from different places. How do you think about the energy in
found objects?

LH   If you look at the works that both of us is doing, they are next door to
the biblical. That means pictorially we are trying to present nothing
else but the truth, no matter how much it hurts us, no matter how sad
we have to be, because I'm sure a young lady like her could have been
out there trying to do something else with her life and not have to just
sit around and nurse her art. Yes, I said "nurse." She is a nurse to the
art that she's creating. She's allowing her thoughts to be cultivated.
I call it thoughtsmithing. Someone said it best, who said "be the best
at what you do." But we have to learn to be the best. All I can say is be
true to what you do. I'm talking to every artist out there: We have to
reshape this mothership where others they can come along on it and
do well.

TL   I hold space for spirits and frequencies because they've always
seemed to be an obvious part of life. In my studio I'm a conductor and
a conduit, and I'm able to receive messages because I'm open to
them. The sensitivity takes me out of commission some days. It's hard
to explain to people, so I don't really try to, but it's not regular lethargy.
Early on in school I was in special education because I didn't want to
speak. They also said I had depression. Words don't always work for
me, and that frustrates me. I don't know what frustrates me more,
humans or words. My dad owned and operated a reggae bar called
Thymeless in Toronto and worked really long nights. But when he
wasn't there, he would isolate in his apartment with the blinds drawn.
He told me he was going to change my bedroom into a meditation
room and paint it all black. It disturbed me back then, but I think I get
it now. Being sensitive is painful, but it's the only way. I did whatever I

could for a while to not feel so much. I went on medications to inhibit my receptors. I had to do the work of helping my mom end her journey on earth but being on autopilot also cut off my access to my spiritual work. I tried to prolong the nonfeeling and still do my work but couldn't. Being receptive and open still is unpredictable and scary. Because nearly everything can make a sound. And it finds its way into your skin. I open myself up to it and I can speak loud and clear with my art. That's my experience. Not everyone needs to experience art in that way, but my work is what it is to me because of sensory receptivity, and a portal that's been there since I was little. I've been steadily sinking back into a flow state, but it feels deeper and more intense because of where I've been at the past couple of years. The messages are burning and beautiful. I've had to block off a part of the studio that's an absolute mess and that's where I figure everything out. Sometimes I struggle with the idea of trying to authenticate myself to people. My art practice is also my spiritual practice, and my studio is where I make sense of things. It can be draining having visitors come through because I have to prepare scaffolding around me and my things. Sometimes I struggle to maintain a holistic view of what it is I do and why, whilst existing in the contemporary art world.

LH But what I try to be is inspiration and motivation for her to get beyond those emotions. Because those emotions, it's like barricades. They are like walls that is put between our endurance and put between what we can accomplish. It takes a lifetime for us to lay our foundation of motivation. If you never ever get a chance to walk in the studios of Atlanta, my studio are where all the other artists that have dead and gone is. They lead us to speak on their behalf. They need us to speak on their behalf. This is my sermon. My art is my sermon. We are in America, trying to find a way out of this jungle. . . . Get to the land of freedom. I love you for being able to be the type of woman you are. There is not better men and women that can impress me.

TL Thank you, Lonnie.

JD In what ways do you both feel called toward certain modes of creating?

TL I recognize that I'm in an early stage of my career, assuming that I keep making art. I've done some damage to my joints and my back to make my sculptures. I feel tired a lot of the time, not even physically, more

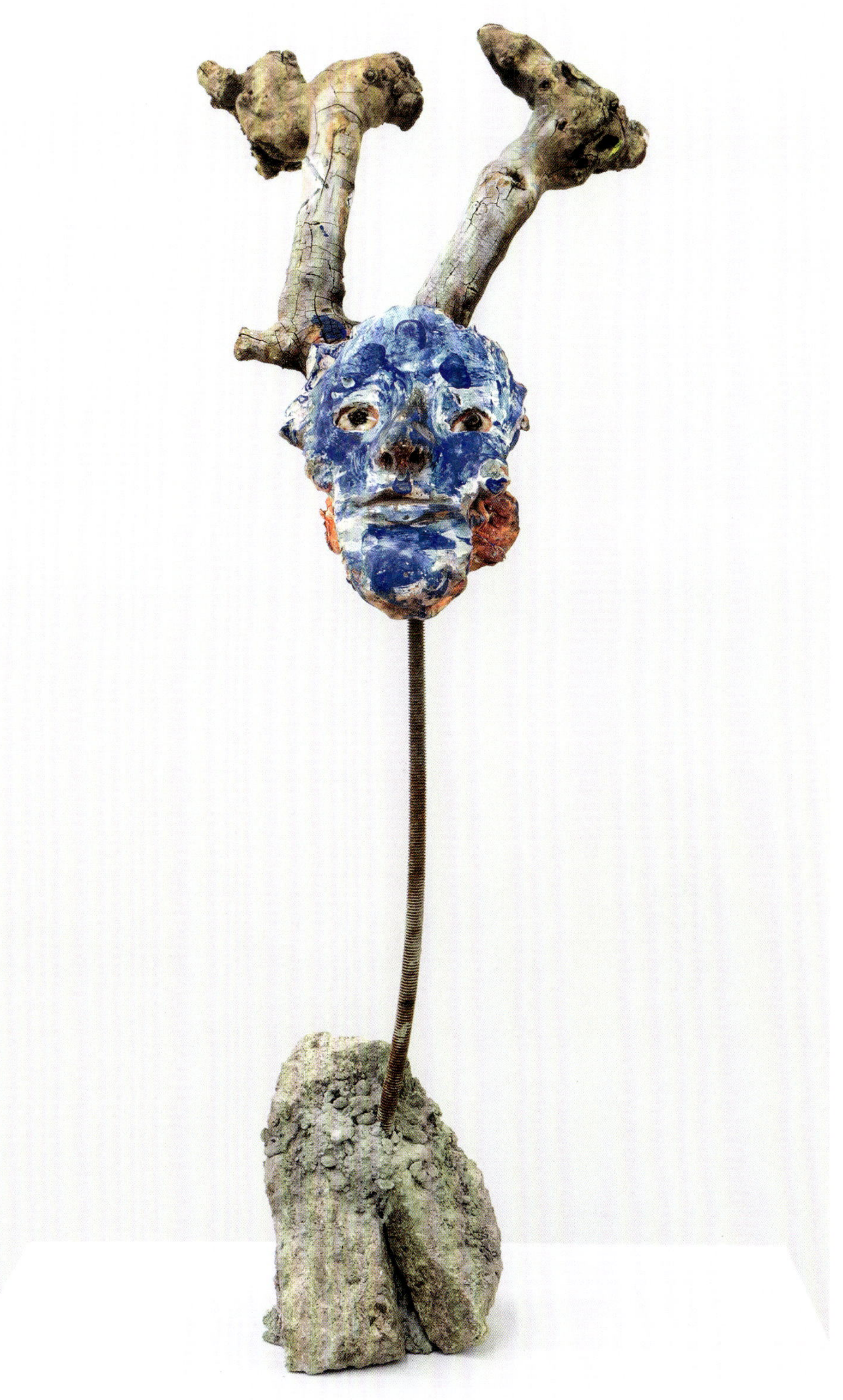

Heartbeat (quiet thrum),
2017. Hand-carved plaster,
seashells, chalk pastel, oil
pastel, acrylic paint, secret
object, wood, rebar, and
concrete. Dimensions
unknown. Collection of
Aimee Friberg

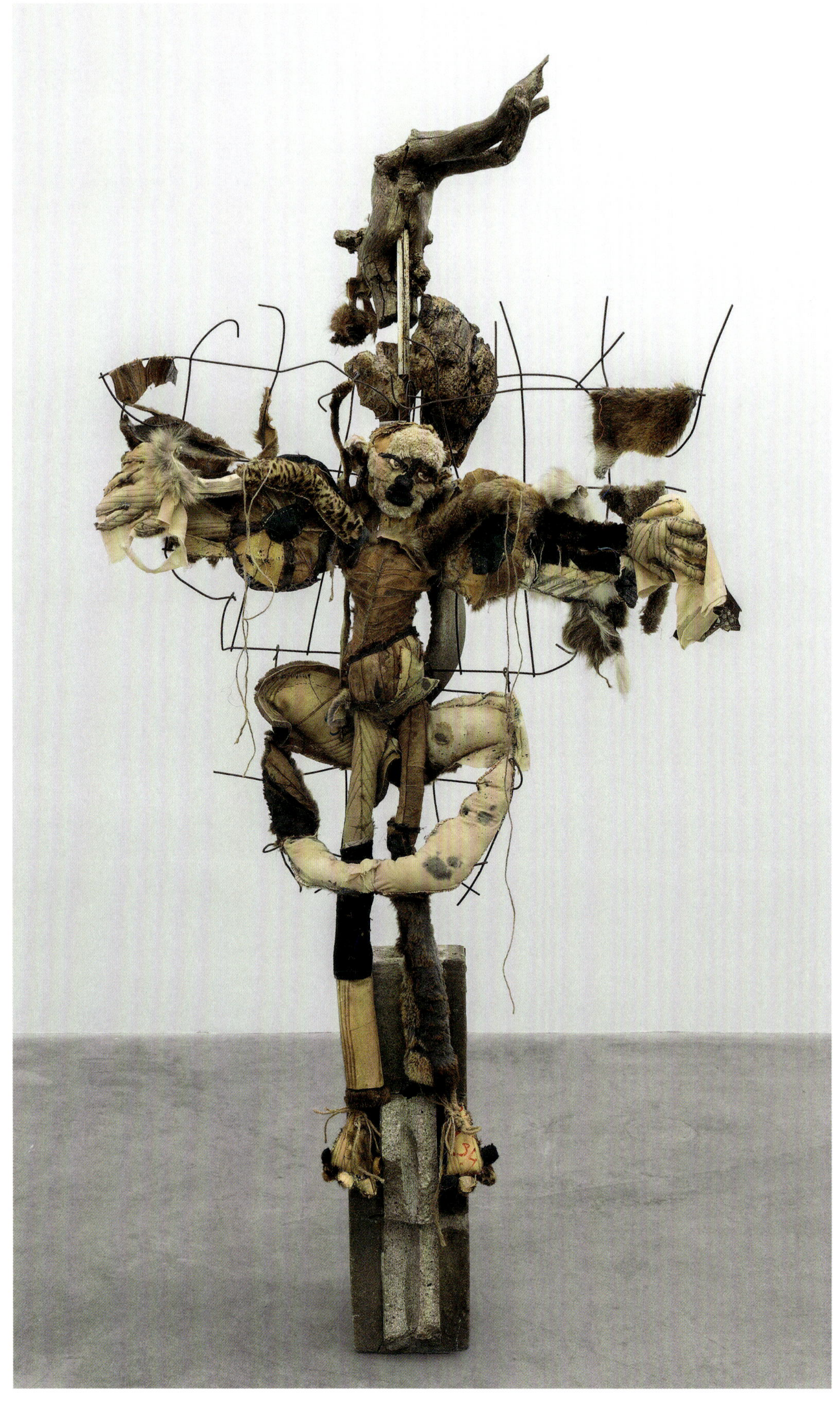

like a pathological fatigue. But this is also the place where I derive the greatest joy and sense of purpose. I feel other avenues are waiting for me on my path. Creation will always be my purpose, I believe everything will unfold in time. I think it's something that Lonnie can definitely speak to because the music is everything right now. And music is a huge part of my life too, I can't exist without it, I can't work without it, I can't dream without it, and so I wonder if the territory of sound is somewhere that I'll go eventually because it is all a vibration. Sculpture is where I live right now.

LH Mine is a calling. These kind of thoughts that I'm about to say bring tears to my eyes. Because we have storms, tornadoes, hurricanes, twisters that come to our daily lives and tear our living structures to pieces. Tear them to smithereens, tear them to bits and particles and small pieces of debris. . . . A lot of us is not thinking to that depth. We're not letting our brain carry us there. It's the ocean of wonder that we allow ourselves to fall into the depths of and this planet and Mother Universe herself has the depths of wonder that we will never be able to think within in our lifetime. But we could help others just by showing them after going through whatever we went through. And I've been through a lot. But look in the mirror, as Michael Jackson say, "man in the mirror." Look at what we're doing to the earth. Look at what we are doing to this planet as humanity. I was not just listening to a Chubby Checker: [*sings*] "Come on, let's twist again like we did last . . . " there may not be another summer, [*sings*] "like we did last summer. Come on, let's twist again like we did last year." It may not be another year. Some storm could come through and wipe out my life, wipe out my existence. Y'all got me trying to preach a sermon this morning and ain't nobody in the audience. I don't have a congregation and I think that's the way Tau feel a lot of times. The people that still *need* to be listening to her is not paying any attention. But let me tell you something, sweetheart: the ones that have to make it possible for it to be futuristic, those are the ones that is paying attention. . . . This conversation will allow us to make that connection. It's almost like we are on this path of righteousness. When I first met her, I was so intrigued with what she was doing, I was trying to make sure that I got enough of me and I got enough of that motivation, that spiritual inspiration sunk into her brain, that would last her until we meet again. And now we are here to spread it throughout the world.

Three angels waiting, 2018. Concrete, rebar, concrete mesh, fur, leather, fabric, cotton batting, stones, pipes, driftwood, dried flowers, and hardware. 76 × 38 × 24 inches (193 × 96.5 × 61 cm). Private collection

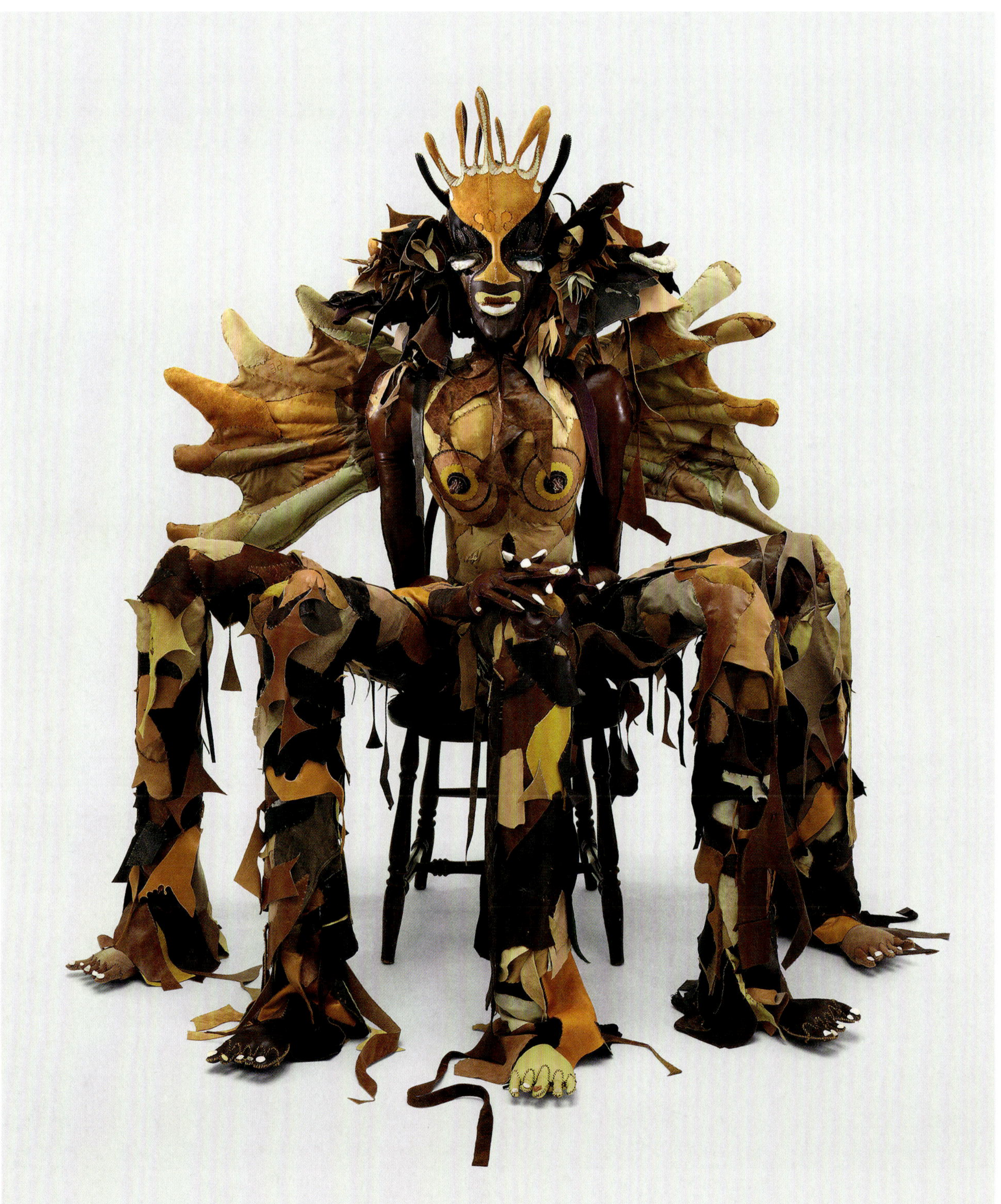

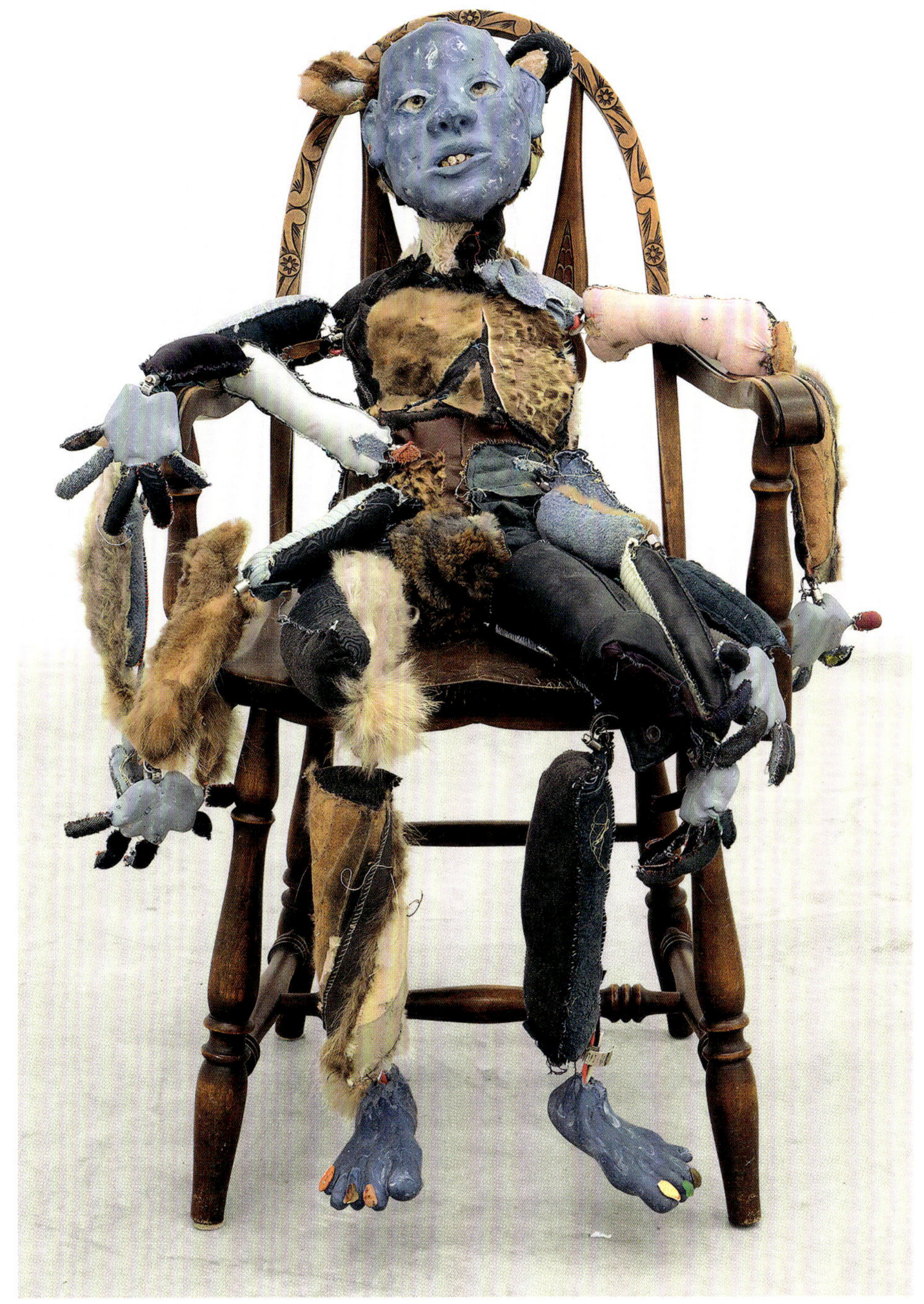

Opposite: *Mater Dei*, 2022. Steel, enamel paint, recycled leather, fur, shearling, suede, tortoise shell, rawhide, organic cotton twill, and coated nylon thread. 134 × 113⅜ × 31 inches (340.4 × 288 × 78.7 cm). Courtesy the artist and 52 Walker, New York

Unity (Negros Historical Information Systems in Every Dark Corner), 2018. Hand-carved plaster, wire, fur, leather, fabric, seashells, stones, cotton batting, polyester batting, human hair, acrylic paint, and chalk pastel. Dimensions variable. Collection of Christine and Murray Quinn

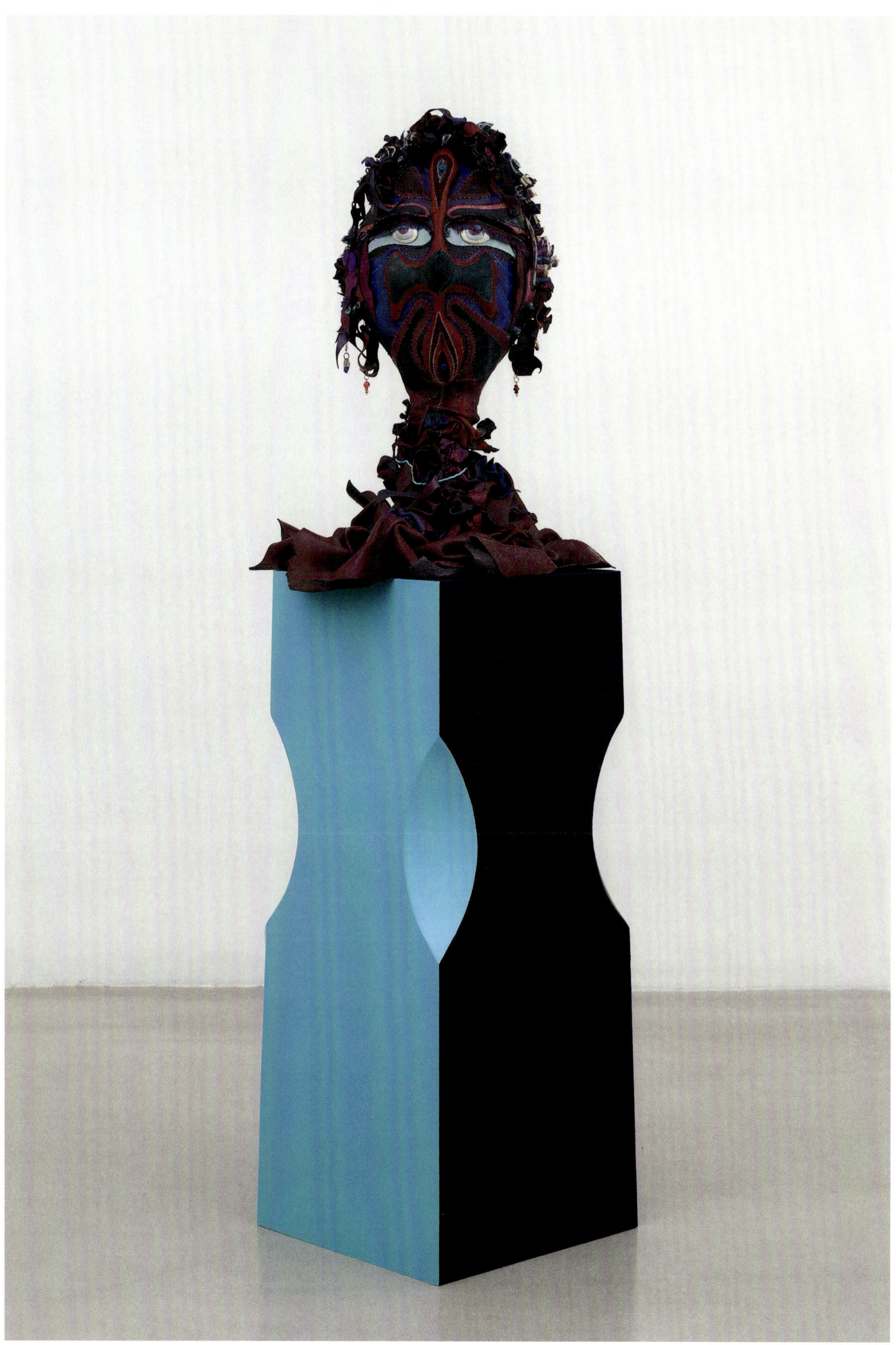

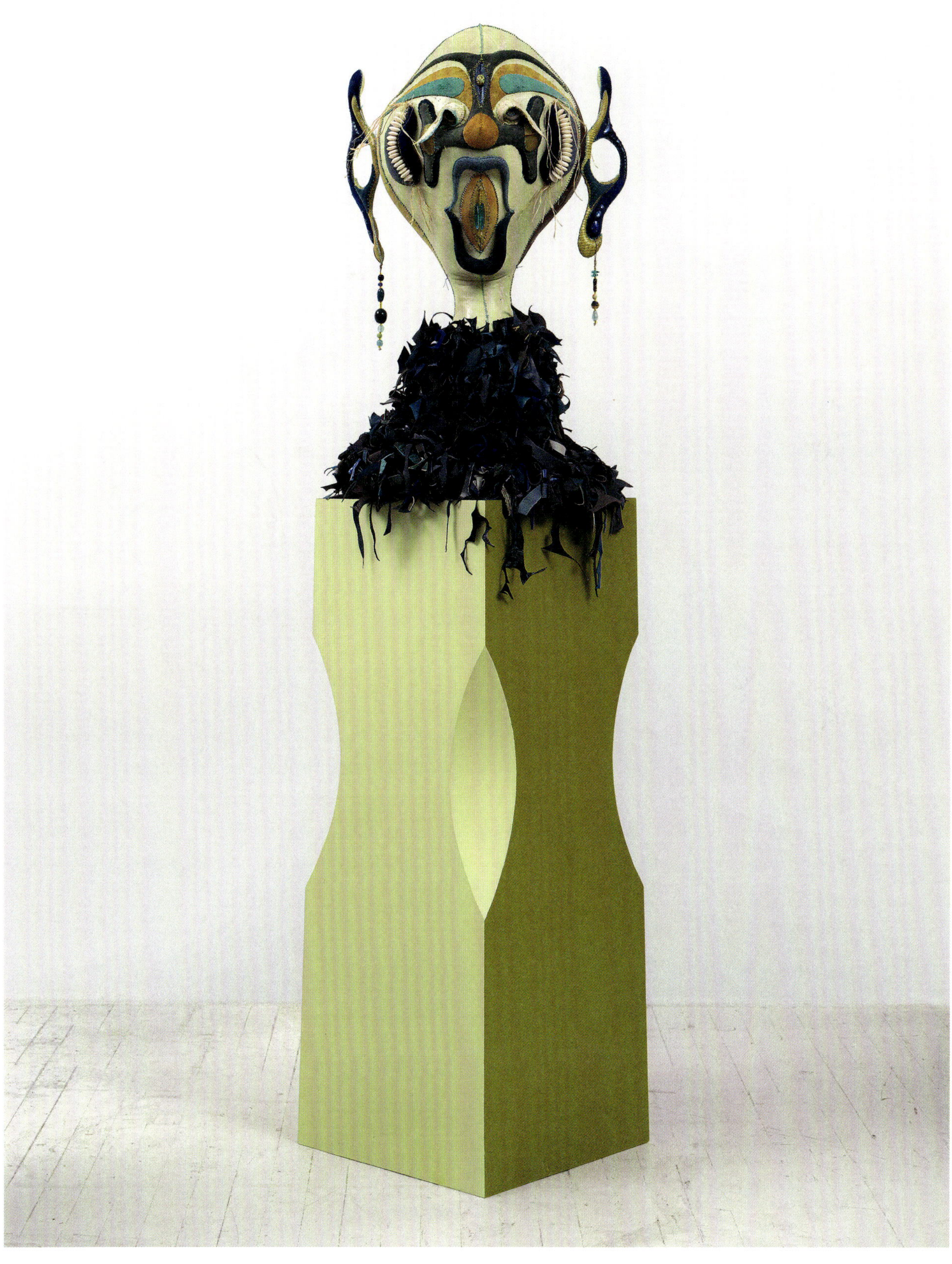

JD How do you both use your art to analyze connectivity? How are the artworks (including music) portals, or points of access through which we can connect with one another?

TL The way that we were found by each other is a good example. Also, while Lonnie was speaking just now, I was remembering some moments we shared at Souls Grown Deep. Matt [Arnett] was there too. We walked around the warehouse together. We spent a good few hours absorbing everything. We took our time and Lonnie guided me. I was seeing parts of him and his life and really meeting his family and friends in the artworks. As we looked at different sculptures, he kept pointing things out. He was reflective and took long pauses. He felt concerned and dismayed that certain materials had been used. He also shared stories of his friends. He broke a corner off one of his sand-stone sculptures and carved me a tiny parrot with his thumbnail. Then we got to the work of Thornton Dial and Lonnie began to sing songs for Mr. Dial. It felt like Mr. Dial was there with us. I just stood there and felt everything. I felt so lucky to be there in that moment. That was a time when we were inside the portal together. I think that everything is aligned for a reason and I think that I make art because I have to and even when it's difficult to do the work, it's just what I have to do.

LH I'm glad that you said I make art because I have to. I make art because I have to. Because I'm interested in making sure through historical infor-mation that there will be enough images. And this is the reason why I be saying something to motivate you. These are the things that we have to tend to. And don't you worry, little sister. Remember, do your work. You are an artist. You've been chosen by the spirit. I've been chosen by the spirit. I am that I am and this is what I'm doing and I will do it until they put me in my grave. But I think I'm here doing a good job. You'll find that I had not and I will not forsake no living person or those that is yet to come. I say thumbs up for Mother Universe!

TL Thumbs up for Mother Universe!

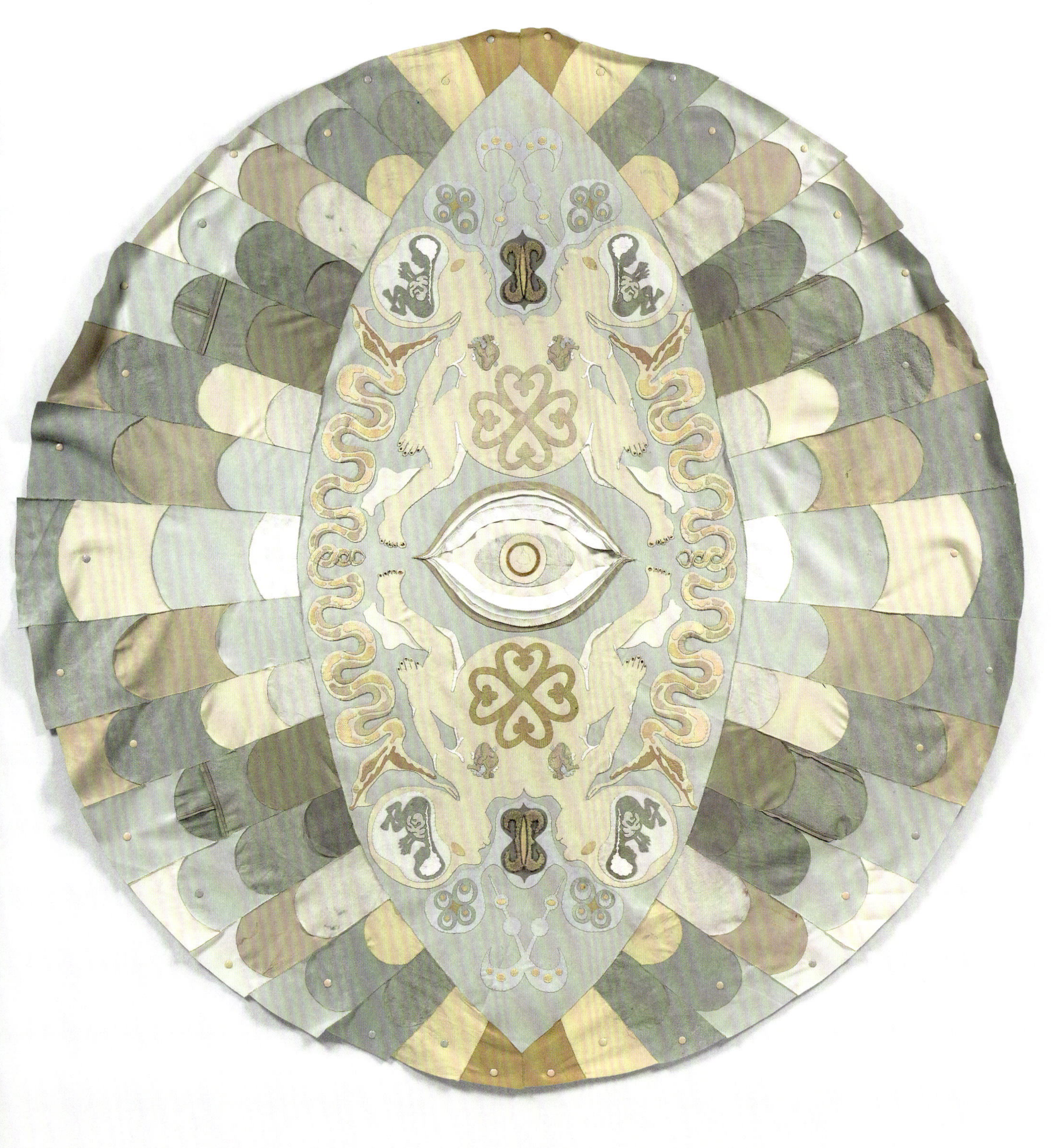

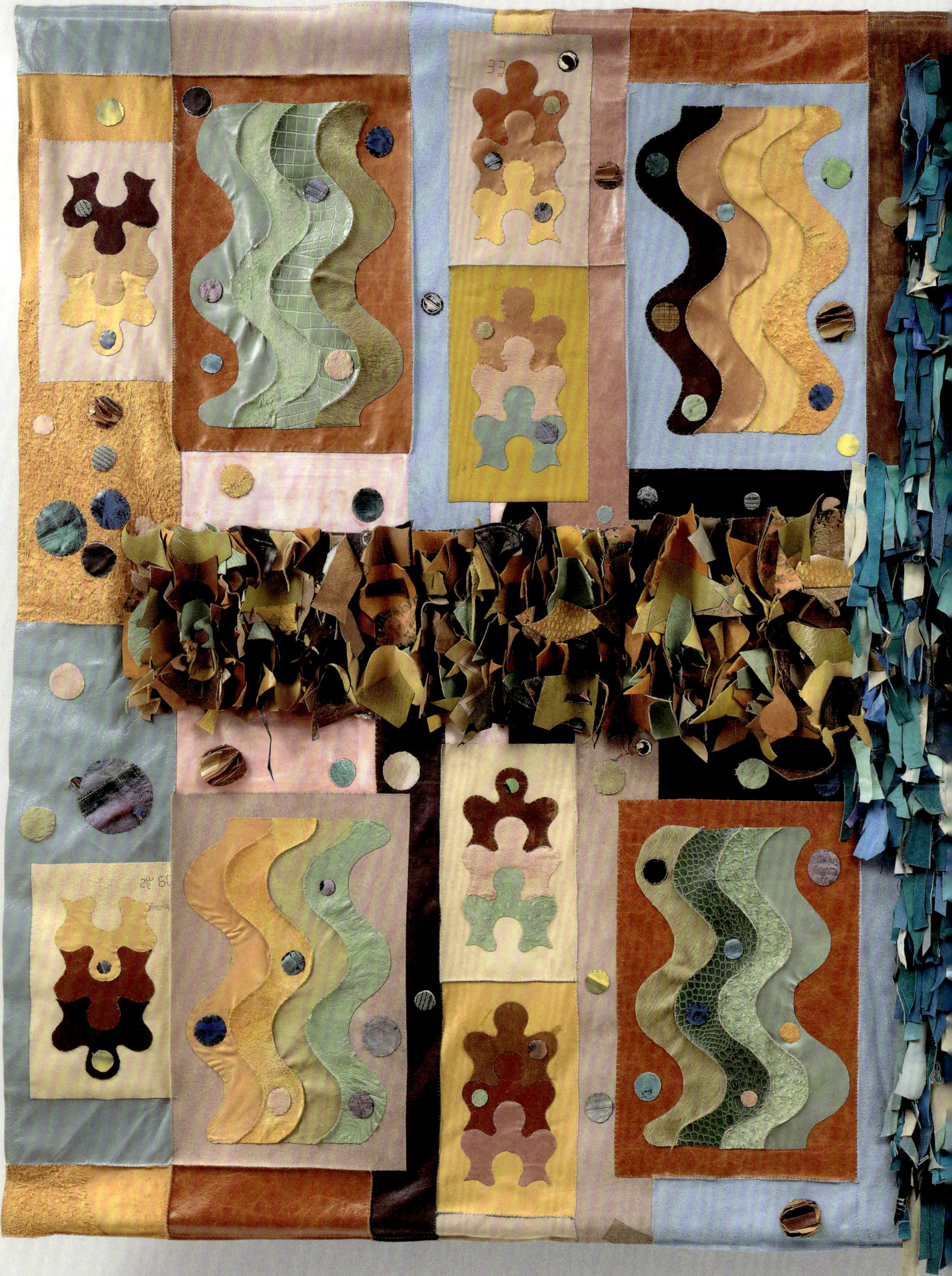

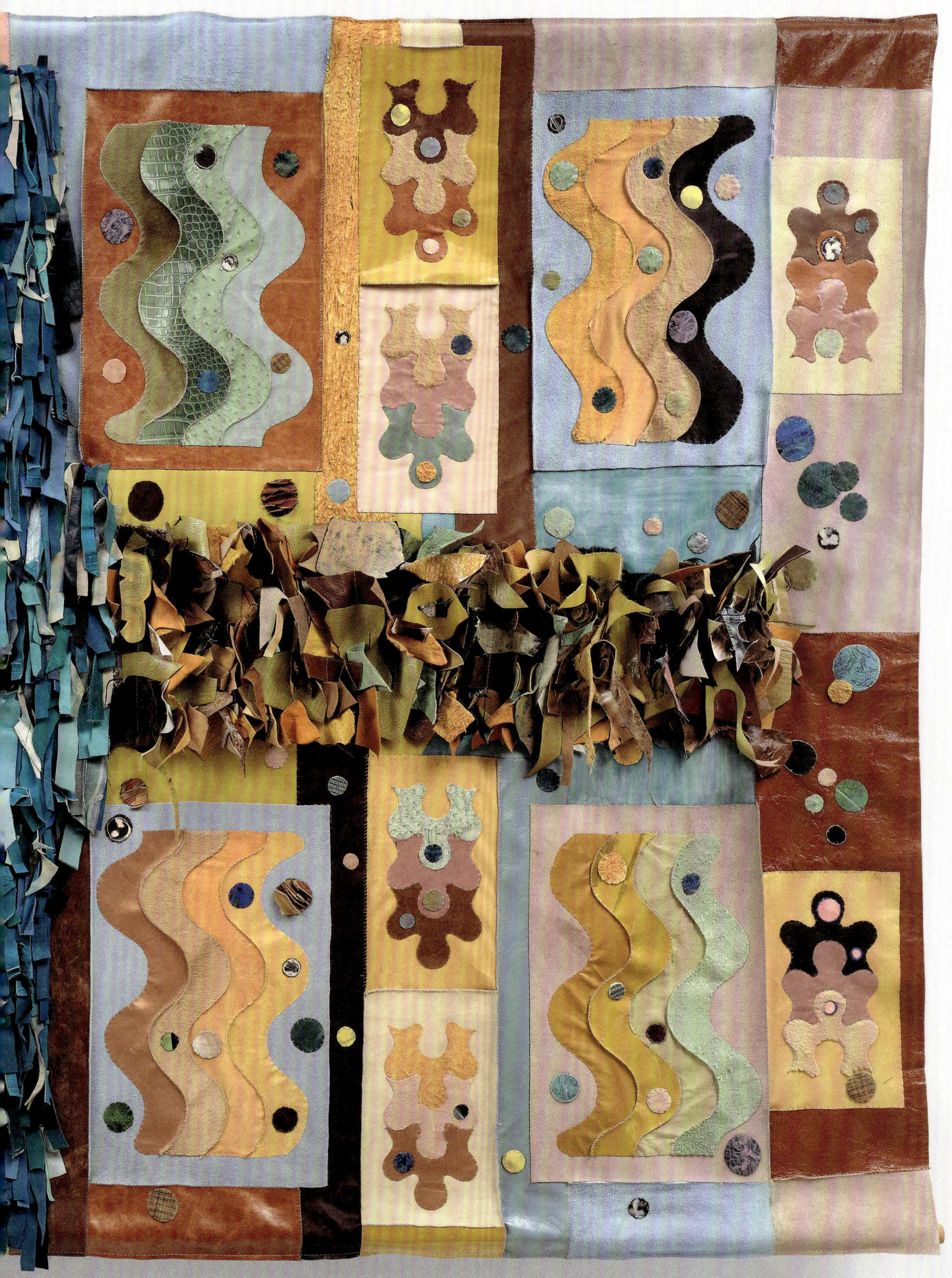

Biography

Born 1993 in Toronto
Lives and works in New York

Solo Exhibitions

2023
Tau Lewis, Institute of Contemporary Art, Miami

2022
Vox Populi, Vox Dei, 52 Walker, New York

2021
Symphony, The National Gallery of Canada, Ottawa, ON
Sparkle's Map Home, Oakville Galleries, ON, Canada

2019
the coral reef preservation society, Yorkshire Sculpture International at The Hepworth Wakefield, UK
when you last found me here, Kenderdine Art Gallery, University of Saskatchewan, Canada

2018
I bet this cave has been here for a really long time, Shoot the Lobster, New York
When you last found me here, The Agnes Etherington Art Centre, Kingston, ON, Canada
Tau Lewis, Atlanta Contemporary

Group Exhibitions

2024
Unravel: The Power and Politics of Textiles in Art, Barbican, London

2023
Making Their Mark, Shah Garg Foundation, New York
The Wedge Collection: Dancing in the Light, Museum of Contemporary Art, Toronto
Au-delà, Lafayette Anticipations, Paris

2022
To Begin Again: Artists and Childhood, Institute of Contemporary Art/Boston
Black Atlantic, Public Art Fund, Brooklyn Bridge Park, Brooklyn, NY
Biennale Arte 2022: The Milk of Dreams, 59th International Art Exhibition, La Biennale di Venezia
Awakening: seeing beyond the frame, Musée d'art de Joliette, Quebec, Canada

2021
The Armory Show, Platform Sector, New York
Yesterday we said tomorrow, Prospect.5, New Orleans
No Humans Involved, Hammer Museum, Los Angeles

2019

Estuary, Nanaimo Art Gallery, BC, Canada
People, Jeffrey Deitch, Los Angeles

2018

RAGGA NYC × Mercer Union, Mercer Union, Toronto

2017

Unmasked, Art Gallery of Mississauga, ON, Canada
RAGGA NYC × PS1 × DIS: *Back to School*, MoMA PS1,
New York
Entering the Landscape, Plug In Institute of
Contemporary Art, Winnipeg, MB, Canada
Migrating the Margins, Art Gallery of York University,
Toronto
Ragga NYC: *All the threatened and delicious things
joining on another*, New Museum, New York
DOORED 29, Art Gallery of Ontario, Toronto
The Un-Othered Body, Ontario College of Art and
Design Graduate Gallery, Toronto

2016

Massive Party 2016: Midnight Massive, Art Gallery of
Ontario, Toronto

2015

Women in Music and Arts, Emmanuel Howard Park
United Church, Toronto
Massive Party 2015: HOTBED, Art Gallery of Ontario,
Toronto

2014

TAVES 2014, Sheraton Centre, Toronto

Permanent Collections

Grinnell College Museum of Art, Grinnell, IA
Hammer Museum, Los Angeles
Institute of Contemporary Art, Miami
Library and Archives Canada, Ottawa, ON
Metropolitan Museum of Art, Library Collection,
New York
Montreal Museum of Fine Arts
National Gallery of Canada, Ottawa, ON
San Francisco Museum of Modern Art

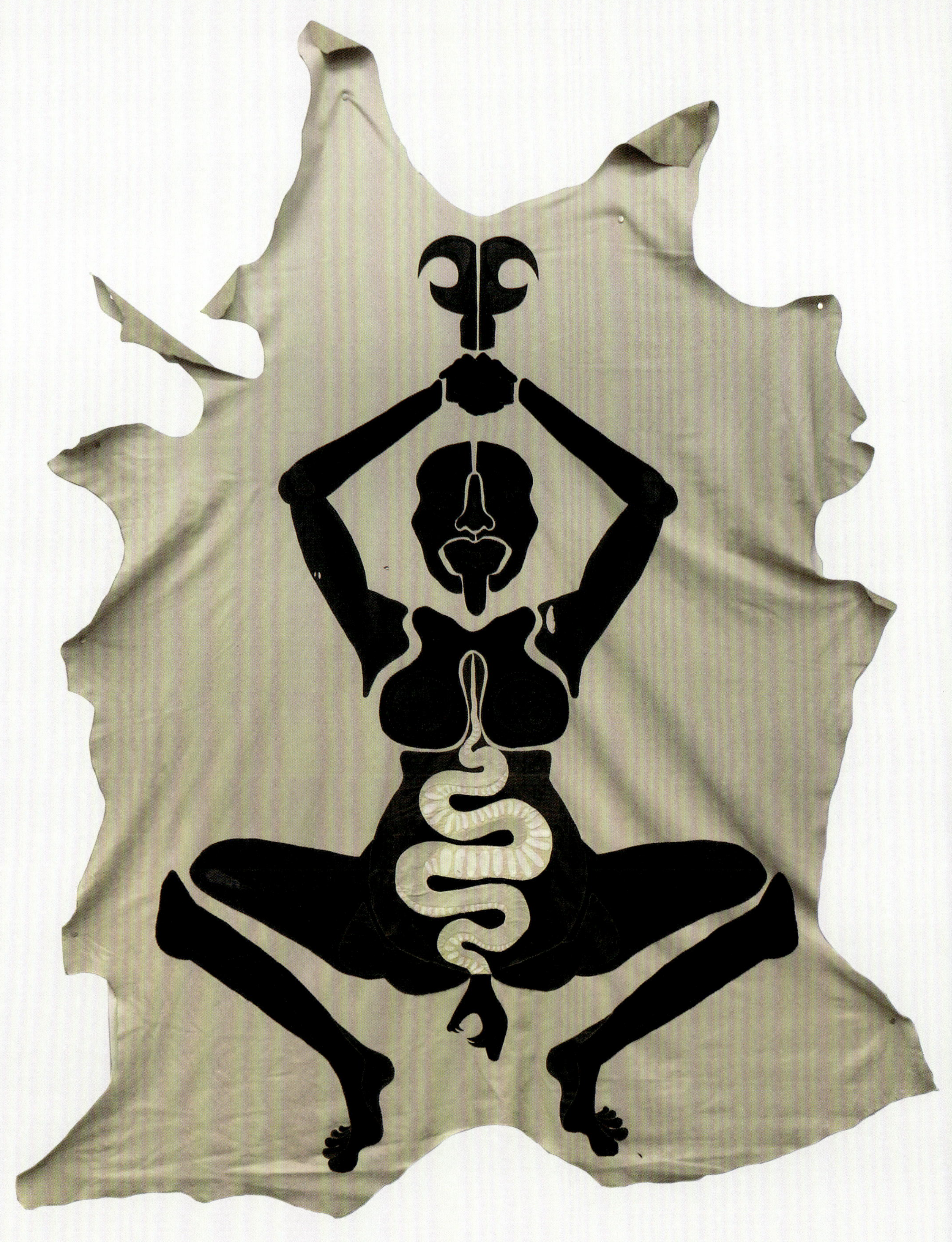

Exhibition Checklist

The Doula, 2024
Steel; enamel paint, acrylic paint, and finisher;
recycled leather, suede, shagreen, and assorted
fabric; leather, fabric, and natural dyes; seashells,
stones, and assorted found objects; coated nylon
thread and coated cotton thread
Approximately 130 × 148 × 148 inches
(330.2 × 375.9 × 375.9 cm)

The Handle of the Axe, 2024
Steel; enamel paint; acrylic paint, and finisher;
recycled leather, suede, shagreen, and assorted
fabric; leather, fabric, and natural dyes; rawhide,
seashells, coral, pearls, stones, and assorted found
objects; beads; coated nylon thread and coated
cotton thread
Approximately 130 × 176 × 148 inches
(330.2 × 447 × 375.9 cm)

The Last Transmission, 2024
Recycled leather and suede; cotton canvas; acrylic
paint and finisher; leather, fabric, and natural dyes;
assorted found metal, wood, ceramic, and glass
objects; wire; beads; seashells; coated nylon thread
and coated cotton thread
Overall diameter approximately 240 inches (609.6 cm)

The Miracle, 2024
Steel; enamel paint, acrylic paint, and finisher;
recycled leather, suede, and assorted fabric; leather,
fabric, and natural dyes; seashells, stones, and
assorted found objects; coated nylon thread and
coated cotton thread
Approximately 130 × 106 × 106 inches
(330.2 × 269.2 × 269.2 cm)

The Night Woman, 2024
Steel; enamel paint, acrylic paint, and finisher;
recycled leather, suede, fur, shagreen, and assorted
fabric; leather, fabric, and natural dyes; cow bone,
conch, stones, and assorted found objects; jute;
coated nylon thread and coated cotton thread
Approximately 130 × 128 × 104 inches
(330.2 × 325.1 × 264.2 cm)

The Reaper, 2024
Steel; enamel paint, acrylic paint, and finisher;
recycled leather, suede, fur, snakeskin, shagreen,
and assorted fabric; leather, fabric, and natural
dyes; seashells, coral, stones, and assorted found
objects; wire; jute; coated nylon thread and coated
cotton thread
Approximately 130 × 148 × 134 inches
(330.2 × 375.9 × 340.4 cm)

All works courtesy the artist

Please note, all information included here is provisional
as these works were in production at time of printing.

The leg of the hen, 2020.
Recycled leather. 108 ×
87 inches (274.3 × 221 cm).
Bill and Christy Gautreaux
Collection. Courtesy the artist
and Night Gallery, Los Angeles

Acknowledgments

After meeting Tau Lewis in 2019, I started thinking of her work in relationship to the group exhibition *To Begin Again: Artists and Childhood* (2022–23) at the ICA, which included her work *Untitled (play dumb to catch wise)* (2017). For Lewis, this sculptural object is actually an embodied subject, a being that has a unique presence in her life. She lives with it and calls it Lil' Gal, describing Lil' Gal as her "most valuable possession." I met Lil' Gal in 2019 at the same time as Lewis, and I say "Hi" every time I'm in the artist's studio. This anecdote only means to suggest that in Lewis's work, as in the work of other artists, I am constantly reminded of the singular importance of art, of the living presence and affirming power it can, and does, hold in our lives. I am extremely grateful to Tau for the unique spirit of collaboration and trust we share, our friendship, and our love for music that is at the heart of it all.

Many people contributed to making Tau Lewis's exhibition at the ICA possible. I am thankful for the transformative support for Lewis's exhibition and publication from Jill Medvedow, Ellen Matilda Poss Director, and Ruth Erickson, Barbara Lee Chief Curator and Director of Curatorial Affairs. I appreciate deeply the early encouragement of Eva Respini, the ICA's former chief curator. The indispensable support of Max Gruber, Curatorial Assistant, made the exhibition and publication possible, and he was a great thought partner and sounding board as everything came into focus. The artist's studio is a special place, and the individuals who support Lewis's work made substantial contributions. Big thanks to Cate Higgins, Studio Manager; Zoe Hochman, Production Manager; Avia Hurley, Art Fair and Inventory Production Lead; and Journey Streams and Brandon Morris, Sewing Assistants. Davida Nemeroff and Rachel Jennings at Night Gallery helped connect all the dots.

This publication benefitted immensely from the contributions of many people. I am so grateful to Lonnie Holley for being in conversation with Lewis, and to Matt Arnett for his incredible support in making the conversation happen. As Lonnie says, "Thumbs up for Mother Universe!" Matthew Christensen brought his sharp eye to bear on the catalogue's texts. I extend my heartfelt thanks to Miko McGinty, Rebecca Sylvers,

Tina Henderson, and Eleanor Morgan at Miko McGinty Inc. who were passionate about making this book a beautifully compelling record of Lewis's creative output from the very beginning. I am always happy to work with the ever-supportive Mary DelMonico of DelMonico Books, who takes this book out into the world for us. On the ICA side, the team of Natasa Vucetic, Chief Financial and Operations Officer, Kelly Gifford, Deputy Director, and Liz Adrian, Director of Retail, are partners in making this book possible. Special thanks to artist and friend Africanus Okokon for ongoing conversations about the influence of dub on visual artists.

I am humbled by the support of the ICA's boards and those who provided generous exhibition support. Thanks to Girlfriend Fund, Robert Nagle and Katherine Hein, Kim Sinatra, the Jennifer Epstein Fund of Women Artists, and Miko McGinty. I am grateful for additional support for this publication from the Fotene Demoulas Fund for Curatorial Research and Publications. The ICA's exhibition team, as always, provided immeasurable support, including Liv Biel, Exhibitions Manager; Emma Blades, Associate Registrar; Charlie Crowell, Preparator; Alison Hatcher, Senior Registrar; Jennifer Ho, Registration Assistant; and Tim Obetz, Chief Preparator. Thanks to Tessa Bachi Haas, Curatorial Assistant, and Erika Umali, Curator of Collections, for being wonderfully enthusiastic colleagues. I am so grateful for ICA colleagues who worked closely with me and Max on different aspects of Lewis's exhibition: Karin France, Director of Institutional Giving; Katrina Bergmann Foster, Director of Development; Monica Garza, Charlotte Wagner Director of Education; Whitney Leese, Chief of Staff and Governance; Colette Randall, Chief Communication and Marketing Officer; Angela Torchio, Principal Designer; and Kris Wilton, Director of Creative Content and Digital Engagement.

At the end of the day, all my work is lovingly supported and embraced by my family. Caty, Jan-Pieter, and Alida, this is dedicated to you.

Jeffrey De Blois
Mannion Family Curator

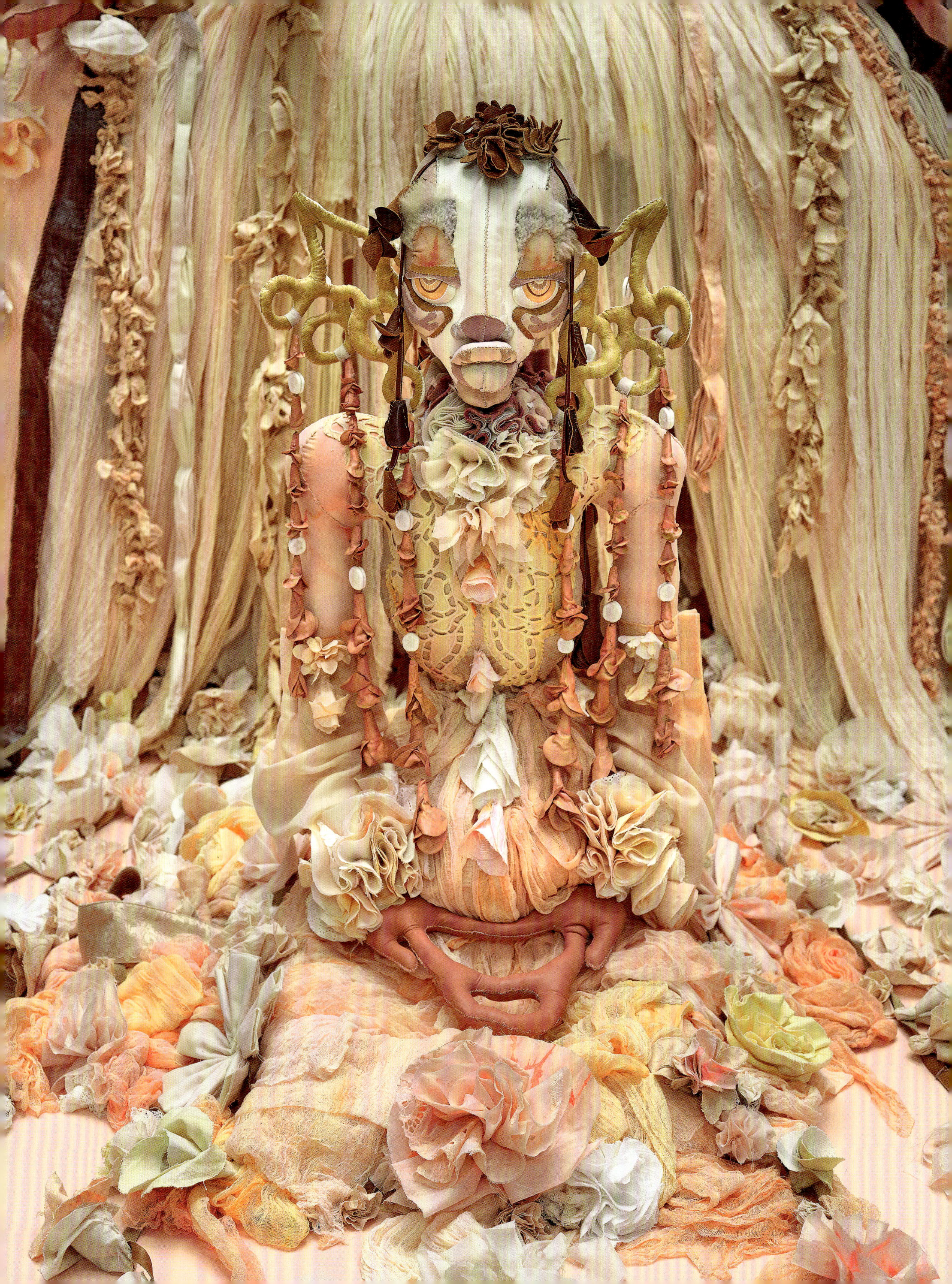

Trustees of the Institute of Contemporary Art /Boston

Symphony (detail), 2019.
Installation view, *Tau Lewis: Symphony*, National Gallery of Canada, Ottawa, 2020–21

This book is published on the occasion of the exhibition
Tau Lewis.

Organized by Jeffrey De Blois, Mannion Family Curator,
with Max Gruber, Curatorial Assistant.

The Institute of Contemporary Art/Boston
August 29, 2024–January 20, 2025

Tau Lewis is supported by Girlfriend Fund, Robert Nagle and
Katherine Hein, Kim Sinatra, the Jennifer Epstein Fund for
Women Artists, and Miko McGinty.

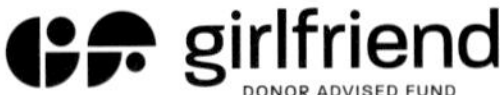

Additional support for this publication is provided by the Fotene
Demoulas Fund for Curatorial Research and Publications.

Published in 2024 by the Institute of Contemporary Art/
Boston and DelMonico Books • D.A.P.

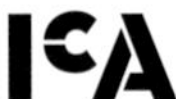

The Institute of Contemporary Art/Boston
25 Harbor Shore Drive
Boston, MA 02210
www.icaboston.org

DelMonico Books
available through ARTBOOK | D.A.P.
75 Broad Street, Suite 630
New York, NY 10004
artbook.com
delmonicobooks.com

Design and production: Rebecca Sylvers and Tina Henderson,
Miko McGinty Inc.
Publication coordinator: Max Gruber
Text editor: Matthew Christensen

Printed in Italy by Conti Tipocolor
Color separations by Prographics

A catalog record for this book is on file with the
Library of Congress

ISBN: 978-1-63681-143-7

All images courtesy the artist unless otherwise indicated.

Front cover: *Vena Cava*, 2021. Steel, recycled leather, acrylic
paint, and coated nylon thread. 121½ × 84 × 43 inches
(308.6 × 213.4 × 109.2 cm). Private collection. Photo by
Frankie Tyska

Frontispiece: *Knot of Pacification* (detail), 2021. Recycled
leather, wool, and suede. 114 × 100 inches (289.6 × 254 cm).
Shah Garg Collection. Courtesy the artist and Night Gallery,
Los Angeles

Table of Contents: *Ascension of the Holy Vessel (Be Not
Afraid)* (detail), 2020. Recycled leather and fabric, acrylic
paint, rawhide, found photographs, found objects, bone,
seashells, and stones. 216 × 108 inches (548.6 × 274.3 cm).
Hammer Museum, Los Angeles. Purchased through the
Board of Advisors Acquisition Fund

pp. 6–7: *Saint Mozelle* (detail), 2022. Steel, enamel paint,
acrylic paint and finisher, recycled leather and suede, organic
cotton twill, and coated nylon thread. 113¾ × 95¼ × 59 inches
(288.9 × 241.9 × 149.9 cm). Courtesy the artist and 52 Walker,
New York. Photo by Maris Hutchinson

p. 8: *Venus in Leo* (detail), 2023. Steel, wood, enamel paint,
acrylic paint, leather dye and finisher, repurposed leather
and suede, repurposed fabric, found jewelry, clam shells, and
coated nylon thread. 68 × 18 × 18 inches (172.7 × 45.7 ×
45.7 cm). Collection of Fotene Demoulas and Tom Coté.
Courtesy the artist, Night Gallery, Los Angeles, and JTT,
New York. Photo by Charles Benton

pp. 10–11: *the coral reef preservation society* (detail), 2019.
Denim, fabric, plaster, and seashells. 180 × 230 inches
(457.2 × 584.2 cm). Love, Luck and Faith Collection

Back cover: *sword of war*, 2020. Handsewn leather. 125¼ ×
110¼ inches (318.1 × 280 cm). Collection of Lonti Ebers.
Courtesy the artist and Night Gallery, Los Angeles

Photo credits
p. 29: Photo by Stephen Pitkin; pp. 36–37, 78: Photos by
NGC; pp. 39–41: Photo by Maris Hutchinson; p. 42: Photo by
Pierre Le Hors; pp. 48–49, 70–71: Photos by Frankie Tyska;
p. 62: Photo by Kerry McFate; p. 64: Photo by Charles Benton;
p. 65: Photo by Justin Craun.